THE AGUE: A H... ....ORY OF INDIGENOUS MALARIA IN CUMBRIA AND THE NORTH

By
Ian D. Hodkinson

CUMBERLAND AND WESTMORLAND
ANTIQUARIAN AND ARCHAEOLOGICAL SOCIETY

Tract Series Vol. 26

Cumberland and Westmorland
Antiquarian and Archaeological Society
Hon. General Editor
Professor Colin Richards

THE AGUE: A HISTORY OF INDIGENOUS

MALARIA IN CUMBRIA AND THE NORTH

TRACT SERIES 26

© Ian D. Hodkinson, 2016.

ISBN 978 1 873124 74 1

Printed by
Titus Wilson & Son, Kendal
2016

CONTENTS

LIST OF ILLUSTRATIONS

PREFACE

I did not set out intentionally to write this book: it just happened. The view from my study, which overlooks the distant Lakeland fells and the more immediate Lyth Valley, with its history of flooding and drainage, often induces moments of quiet thought. As a former professional ecologist, I was alert to the current debate on the possible re-establishment of mosquito-transmitted ague (vivax malaria) in the UK, resulting from a warming climate. More parochially, I became aware of proposals by the Environment Agency effectively to re-wet the Lyth Valley by curtailing the pumping operations that maintained a low water table. I lived for a while in Ormskirk, on the fringe of a similar large drained wetland, Martin Mere, on the Lancashire coastal plain. Malaria was historically endemic within that area but disappeared in the 19th century, largely as a result of large-scale drainage that removed the mosquitoes' aquatic breeding habitat. While sitting in my study on a particularly wet summer's day staring at puddled fields, I started musing on the possibility of malaria re-establishing in South Lakeland. This stimulated me to start looking, initially in a perfunctory way, at the historical evidence for ague in Cumbria. I soon discovered that a hidden story was there to unravel and that ague had been much more widespread than I expected, not just in Cumbria but elsewhere in the north. Without quite realising it, my pursuits developed into an obsession that rapidly led me into unfamiliar territory and a very steep learning curve on how to find and extract historical information. This book, based on my researches, represents a short account of my discoveries that I hope will prove accessible and interesting to a wide readership. Such research would have been nigh impossible just ten years ago: I have been continually amazed at the increasing availability of online copies of old books, journals, documents and records and at the ability of search engines to locate the word 'ague' in the most unlikely places – even if it is within words like 'colleague' or 'Montague'.

ACKNOWLEDGEMENTS

I thank wholeheartedly the many people who have assisted me, a biologist by training, to find my stumbling way through the highly-dispersed historical literature and archive material relating to the ague. Sylvia Kelly and Jackie Fay (Cumbria Local Studies Library, Kendal), have, as always, provided unfailing help in locating information and Stephen White has generously sent me images of documents in Carlisle Library. Several archivists have provided their expertise and help and have often identified or sent me highly relevant source information. These include Victoria McCann (Lancashire Archives, Preston), Alison Hurst (Whitehaven Archives), Steven Davies (Flintshire Record Office) and Paul R Ternent (Northumberland Archives). Katherine Marshall (Royal Society) provided a copy of the Duke of York's report on malaria in Scotland. Rachel Roberts (Museum of Lakeland Life & Industry) provided the image of a quinine bottle and John Betts (Royal Pharmaceutical Society Museum) hunted out the image of an original Daffy's Elixir bottle. Ken Howarth kindly agreed to the publication of the image of St Agnes Well from the *The Heritage Photo Archive and Heritage Image Register*. Lady Judith le Fleming and Keswick Congregational Church generously gave permission to publish the illustrations, held by Cumbria Archives, of the treatments for ague shown in Fig. 12 respectively. Dr Jonathan Healey (University of Oxford) provided guidance and suggestions in relation to the Poor Law in NW England and Prof. Angus Winchester (Lancaster University) supplied information, particularly relating to Isaac Fletcher of Underwood. Stephen Read kindly commented on an early draft and made several helpful suggestions. Publication of this book was supported by grants from The Royal Entomological Society of London Outreach Fund, The Hadfield Trust, Levens Charity and Levens Local History Group.

Finally, I acknowledge my gratitude to the many freely-available data sources now available online: even ten years ago work of this nature, drawing on such disparate and diffuse resources, would have been nigh impossible. I owe a particular debt to *Internet Archive, The Haithi Trust Digital Library, The National Archives* and *The British Newspaper Archive*.

Introduction

From his obscure haunt
Shriek'd FEAR, of Cruelty the ghastly Dam,
Fev'rish yet freezing, eager paced yet slow,
As she that creeps from forth her swampy reeds,
Ague, the biform Hag! When early Spring
Beams on the marsh bred-vapours.

Samuel Taylor Coleridge
A Destiny of Nations

.....Both hot and cold, the heartaches every day, –
How hard alas! To bear, I only know.

Such shaking doth the fever in my keep
Throughout all this May that I have little sleep;....

William Wordsworth
The Cuckoo and the Nightingale

Malaria, commonly known as the ague or marsh fever, was well known to the Lake Poets, as it inflicted seasonal misery on both the rural and urban inhabitants of Westmorland, Cumberland and Lancashire North of the Sands. This book examines the nature and historical extent of the ague within this local area and beyond, and the reasons for its disappearance. It describes the place of the ague in rural folklore and documents the methods, both efficacious and fanciful, for its treatment. It concludes by examining the possibility of ague becoming re-established in its former haunts.

Ague, as we shall see, was at one time widespread in Britain, attracting the attention of other writers including Charles Dickens, who inflicted the disease on several of his characters but who also commissioned a serious article entitled 'Ague and its Causes' for the magazine *All the Year Round*, which he edited (Dickens 1868). Oliver Cromwell is said to have died of '... a double tertian ague' (Harris 1762). As early as 1623 Gervaise Markham in his *Countrey Contentments or the English Huswife* lists the recognition of the various

1

forms of ague among his '... inward and outward virtues which ought to be in a compleate Woman' (Markham 1623).

Much that has been written about malaria in Britain has focused on the incidence of the disease in undoubted hotspots such as the fenlands of Lincolnshire, Cambridgeshire, Norfolk and Suffolk, and in the Kent and Essex marshes during the seventeenth and eighteenth centuries (MacArthur 1952, Shute and Maryon 1974, Dobson 1980, 1989, 1994, 1998a,b, Nicholls 2000, Hutchinson and Lindsay 2006). There is abundant evidence, however, that ague was much more broadly distributed within the British Isles than some of the recent literature might suggest. The afflictions of the working poor in more remote rural areas of Britain tended to escape the written attentions they received in more populous areas closer to London. Largely rural areas, such as present-day Cumbria, Wales, lowland Lancashire and the whole of Scotland, are good examples where the wider occurrence of the disease is far less well researched than elsewhere (e.g. Finlay 1978, 1980, Risse 2005).

Ague is a remarkable example of a widespread disease that went into a decline in Britain, almost inadvertently, before its true cause and nature were fully understood. It was not until 1897 that Sir Ronald Ross demonstrated that female blood–feeding mosquitoes were the vectors responsible for transmitting the disease from human to human (Ross 1897). Subsequent to this discovery, just 566 cases were noted between 1917 and 1952, predominantly in rural areas of Kent and Essex (Shute 1954). Today, a combination of climate change, coupled with proposals to re-saturate former low-lying marshy areas in several areas of Cumbria, together with changes in agricultural practice, raises the spectre of malaria possibly re-establishing in its former breeding grounds (Snow 1999, Lindsay and Thomas 2001, Ramsdale and Gunn 2005, Snow and Medlock 2006, Lindsay et al. 2010, Medlock and Vaux 2011).

What is the ague?

Ague is caused by the protozoan parasite *Plasmodium vivax* that infects the liver and the red blood corpuscles of humans and is transmitted by female mosquitos of the genus *Anopheles* (fig.1). The parasite is capable of rapidly reproducing in both its human and insect host.

The symptoms of the ague and similar malarial diseases reflect the duration of the life-cycle of the parasite within the human body, inducing alternating periods of intense cold-feeling and shivering or shaking followed by a high fever, usually over a three to four day cycle, hence the name *tertian* or *quartan* ague. A patient can suffer several successive bouts of debilitating fever and the disease may persist in the body for several months before symptoms first appear. Severe cases result in damage to the spleen and death. Ague *per se* does not cause pathological lesions on skeletal remains but it causes hemolytic

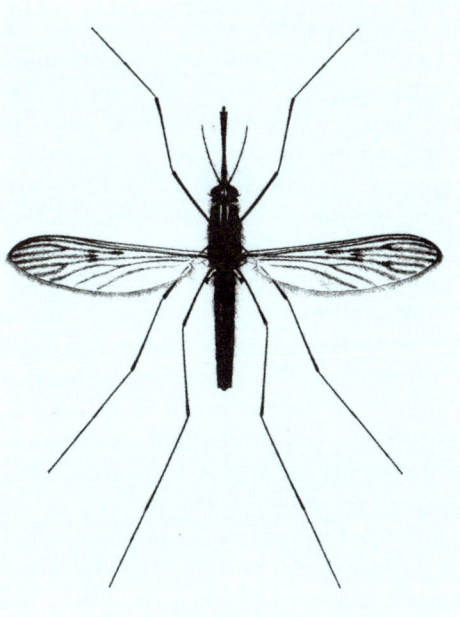

Fig.1. Female *Anopheles* 'maculipennis' type mosquito. Note the long proboscis that is used to draw blood from the host. (Reproduced from William Lang's *British Mosquitoes*, 1920).

anaemia, which can contribute to a skeletal condition known as criba orbitalia. It has been suggested that a high incidence of this condition (10-34 per cent) among Anglo-Saxon skeletons from malarial areas in eastern England is indicative of infection by the ague (Gowland and Western 2012). Because of its persistent and cyclical nature, ague was often referred to as intermittent or remittent fever.

The mosquito vectors of ague and their distribution

Six potential malaria-carrying species of *Anopheles* mosquito, namely *algeriensis*, *atroparvus*, *claviger* (= *bifurcatus*), *daciae*, *messeae* and *plumbeus*, occur in Britain (Cranston et al. 1987, Snow 1998, Danabalan et al. 2014). *Anopheles daciae*, a close relative of *A. messeae*, was only recognised as a distinct species in Britain in 2005, from specimens collected on the Somerset Levels (Linton et al. 2005). Several of the *Anopheles* species are difficult to separate, except by using molecular techniques, and *atroparvus*, *messeae* and almost certainly *daciae* were for a long time confused under a single species called *A. maculipennis* (e.g. Nuttall et al. 1901, Lang 1918, Snow 1998). Consequently, they were not until recently recorded as separate species (Snow 1998, Linton et al. 2005). This old combined '*A. maculipennis*' has been found as far north as the Grampian region in Scotland (Cranston et al. 1987, Snow 1998). The precise identity of the historic malaria vector(s) in Cumbria and the north is thus, for several reasons, uncertain. *A. 'maculipennis'*, *claviger* and *plumbeus* are recorded from Cumbria and *messeae* is known from Cheshire, Yorkshire and Northumbria (Snow 1998, Linton et al. 2005). By contrast, *A. algeriensis* is known only from the south-east of England and *A. daciae* is currently recorded as a southern species, known from as far north as Anglesey (Snow 1998, Danabalan et al. 2014). The present recorded distribution of *A. atroparvus* is predominantly in southern England as far north as Cheshire, leaving the true identity of the northern '*maculipennis*' species uncertain (Linton et al. 2005, Danabalan et al. 2014a). The problem is confounded by the fact that when malaria was rife in Cumbria its association with mosquitoes was unknown and no systematic collecting of potential insect vectors took place. We can thus only surmise which mosquito species were involved.

Anopheles species generally breed in shallow standing water (fig. 2) (Cranston et al. 1987). Eggs, which are equipped with a float mechanism, are laid on the water surface. The hatching larvae are free-living in the water column and return to the surface to replenish their oxygen supply, an adaptation that limits the depth of water in which they can live. There are four similar larval stages, the final one of which develops into a pupa. The adult mosquitos emerge from the pupa at the water surface. The rate of development of eggs, larvae and pupae is determined primarily by temperature with development

Fig.2. Typical breeding area of *Anopheles* mosquitoes on the South Lakeland mosslands with open areas of shallow standing water.

often ceasing during winter. Overwintering can occur in either the late larval or adult stage, depending on the species involved.

The current known distribution for all *Anopheles* species combined, based on current data from Biodiversity Network, UK, is shown in (fig. 3). This map, based on the recorded presence of mosquitoes in 10km grid squares, should be interpreted with the following caveats. Only positive records are marked and the lack of a record for a grid square does not necessarily indicate that mosquitoes are absent: the map to some extent represents the intensity of collecting effort in particular areas. Records within Cumbria tend to be concentrated around the southern fringe of the county and around Carlisle and the Eden valley, areas known formerly to have significant malarial presence (see later). The different mosquito species, however, vary in their biology and this may indicate that different species were responsible for transmission in different areas and at separate times. For example, *A. claviger* and *A. plumbeus* tend to be the common species in Scotland (Ashworth 1927). Species may also occur concurrently in the same habitat, such as *A. atroparvus and messeae,*

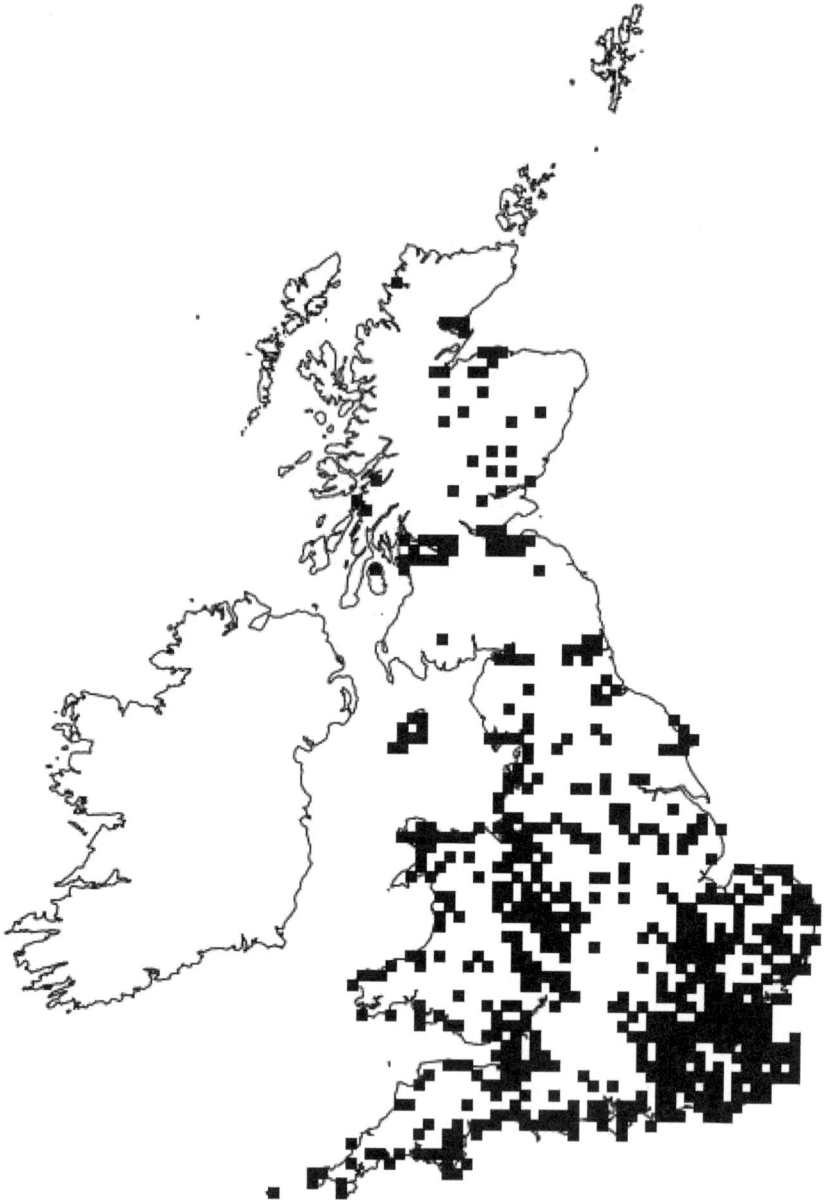

Fig. 3. Map showing the combined distributions of the six species of *Anopheles* mosquito known to occur in the UK (Courtesy of the UK National Biodiversity Network).

either together, or individually with *A. daciae* (Linton et al. 2002, Danabalan 2010, Danabalan et al. 2014). The first two are both warm-adapted species that usually breed in open habitats, including ditches, drains, sluggish streams, ponds, lake edges and marshes (Cranston et al. 1987, Snow 1998, Danabalan 2010). *Anopheles atroparvus* also tolerates high salinities and is suspected of being the main malaria vector in south-east England during the early twentieth century (Shute 1954). *A. claviger*, another proven potential vector is, by comparison, a cool-adapted species that occupies a similarly broad range of habitats that includes water tanks, rain barrels and saline habitats (Blacklock and Carter 1920, Snow 1998). It is widely distributed throughout England, Wales and Scotland (Snow 1998). Breeding sites, however, tend to be shaded and thus cooler. *A. plumbeus*, another similarly widespread species with a proven ability to transmit *P. vivax*, is particularly associated with forests where it breeds in rain-filled tree holes (Blacklock and Carter 1920, Shute 1954, Cranston et al. 1987, Snow 1998). Adult females of all the above *Anopheles* species are known to enter and/or rest within buildings where they may encounter and feed on domestic animals or humans. Several of the species are also known opportunistic feeders on wild animals such as birds and deer (Danabalan 2010, Danabalan et al. 2014). *A. atroparvus* is particularly noted for overwintering in unheated buildings associated with human occupation.

The past distribution of ague in Britain and Ireland

The distribution of ague and the accompanying patterns of high seasonal mortality in the fens and marshes of south-east England are, as already noted, well documented and require little elaboration here (see Creighton 1894, MacArthur 1952, Dobson 1980, 1989, 1998a,b, Nicholls 2000, Hutchinson and Lindsay 2006). Ague, however, was not restricted to the fens; pockets of infection of varying persistence were to be found throughout Britain at different times. The evidence, however, is poorly collated and the information in this section presents, perhaps for the first time, a broader picture of the distribution of ague in Britain, to set the scene for a more detailed exploration of the disease in Cumbria.

To understand the distribution of ague we must piece together a highly-scattered literature in which much of the evidence is anecdotal or forms part of shared folk recollection. Such evidence can be gleaned from guides, histories, diaries, court records and newspapers, together with more localised accounts of life in specific towns or areas. Care is needed to distinguish between ague and the other fever-producing infections prevalent at the time including cholera, typhus, typhoid, plague and scarletina. In assembling the evidence I have only accepted data where the disease has been named or where the symptoms have been clearly defined, particularly the alternating cold-shaking and high fever, or the disease's persistent and intermittent characteristics. The disappearance of the disease, following the drainage of wetlands or treatment with quinine, also serves as a good indicator. In the absence of detailed pathological data, however, we can never be absolutely certain that all cases described were true malaria.

Ague occurred historically in north Lancashire, south of Morecambe Bay, such as at Kirkham, Layton near Blackpool and the area around Garstang (Leigh 1700, Nuttall et al. 1901, Gill 1921, James 1929, Dobson 1980). Hopkins (1839) noted that '... I have been informed by Dr. Briggs of Ambleside ... that in his younger days autumnal agues were common on the low grounds of Lancashire, particularly in that part called the Fylde country, and that they occasionally prevail at present. Their diminution may be attributed to better drainage'.

A series of seventeenth-century painted glass panels described from Hale Hall, just north of Kirkham, represents the four seasons, with winter symbolised by an old man with ague (Nelson 1937):

> ...in age an ague couldnes still we hav[e]
> First stoopi[ing] to the fire then to the grave

An early eighteenth-century handbill, announcing the visit of the quack practitioner Edward Green to Kirkham, lists ague among the diseases he claimed to cure (Fessler 1950). A petition to Lancashire Quarter Sessions, dated around 1705, requests '... relief for Jane and Elizabeth Willson [of Barnacre near Garstang] with Kentish ague'.[29] ★ Another letter, from Alexander Rigby of Middleton to his brother George Rigby of Peel Hall, Little Hulton, in 1631 mentions several cases of ague among relatives and friends.[26] The letter expresses fear of the plague extending up beyond Garstang and mentions his brother, a member of a well-known legal family, staying with him during assizes week. This strongly suggests that the Middleton in question is the one between Heysham and Overton to the west of

★ Superscript numerals refer to the primary sources listed in the references

Lancaster, where the assizes were held. A humorous poem, published in the *Lancaster Gazette* from a gentleman at Carnforth in 1805, hints strongly that ague was well known in the Lancaster area at the time. It reads:

> ... While thou to Lancaster wer't marching,
> Where Father Sol is seldom parching,
> Where all the female sex are witches,
> And agues spring from fens and ditches...
>
> 'Dick Summers' (1805)

By contrast, there is little to indicate that ague was common in the Isle of Man. Quayle (1812), in his *General View of the Agriculture* on the island, ventured so far as to suggest that '... the ague [was] unknown'.

Ague was at one time common in the parishes of Rufford and Croston, adjacent to the old Martin Mere and Ribble marshes (Redding et al. 1842, Baines 1886, Tyrer 1968-72, Dobson 1994, Chin and Welsby 2004). Baines writes of Rufford that '... the ague formerly prevailed in this parish and district to a considerable amount, but the drainage of the land ... has almost banished that complaint'. Sporadic death from ague is recorded in the parish of North Meols (now in Southport), a short distance from Rufford (Virgoe 2005) and a recipe for an ague cure can be found in the Hawkshead-Talbot archive from Chorley in 1728.[25] In nearby Halsall, a petition for relief in 1642 for Cuthbert Frith, linen weaver, states that he was suffering from '... tertian ague and feaver'.[28] Baines later mentions that Dr Leigh (as in Leigh 1700 above) was one of the first to use Peruvian bark to treat ague in Lancashire, a practice that was said '... to have been attended with great success' (Baines 1867).

Ague was also prevalent at Castle Croft, near Bury on the marshland around the Irwell (Waugh 1892) and is recorded as a cause of death in Deane, near Bolton, during the seventeenth century (Sparke 1917). Dr Richard Kay records attending a patient with ague at Baldingstone near Bury and much later the Bury Union Workhouse Admission Registers occasionally listed ague as a cause of admission between 1864 and 1907 (Brockbank and Kenworthy 1968, [22]). A series of letters from Urmston, Manchester by the Revd Peter Walkden records that '... the small pox and shaking ague were very rife ...' and he notes that his own wife '... had five or six fits [of ague]' (Bromley 1885). Extracts from the diaries of a Lancashire clergyman who spent most of his ministry in Chipping, Lancashire, in the early 1700s note that '... The land was undrained and a large part uncultivated ... as a consequence of the want of drainage and the neglect of sanitary arrangements ... the ravages of epidemics as fevers and agues were frequent' (Bromley 1879-80). Another petition for relief, dated 1642, implicates Ashton in Makerfield, near Warrington, as an ague area lying adjacent to the lowlands along the River Mersey.[27] A more general mention of ague in low-lying areas of Wirral, along the Mersey and Dee, is given by Sanders (1771) in his *Complete English Traveller* who stated that the land '... being extremely low, the people are often afflicted with agues'. Sporadic records of ague can be found in County Durham (Jackson 1809). Bailey (1813), in his *General View of the Agriculture of the County of Durham*, recorded that the area was '... in general very healthy, except a tract of flat country towards the Tees Mouth, which is subject to agues'. The lower parts of the town of Darlington also suffered from intermittent fevers and agues, which disappeared following improvements to the land (Longstaffe 1854). Ague also appears to have made a sporadic appearance in areas of the Durham coalfield (Anon 1853b).

We also do not have to look far for similar examples from Yorkshire, particularly in the old East Riding of Yorkshire. Leatham (1794), in his *General View of the Agriculture of the East Riding of Yorkshire*, recorded that '... Before the present main drains were made in the eastern part of the Riding, a very large proportion of the inhabitants were afflicted with the ague'. Thomas Baines in his *Yorkshire Past and Present* described areas of Holderness as '... a profitless morass, producing ague in the neighbouring district' (Baines 1871). Early family diaries from the 1740s, such as that of James Fretwell, record the impact of the disease on individual families in this region (Jackson 1877). Further west, ague also occurred in the flatlands of lower Swaledale in the North Riding. Correspondence between Joseph Pease of Morton upon Swale and his brother-in-law Ambrose Barcroft of Foulrigg (= Foulridge) in 1668/9 indicate the prevalence of the disease.[24] One letter informs Barcroft that '... Gracy [his sister-in-law] is sharply handled in an ague', another that it is 'a very sickly time in this country, most people generally being afflicted either with colds or agues'. A petition for relief for the family of Anne Askwith of Clint '... in an ague' suggests that the disease was also present along the River Nidd.[31]

Moving further south in England, sporadic evidence for ague can be found in Derbyshire. For example, the late seventeenth-century Snelston Manor Court Book contains a copy of a letter from the deserted wife of William Bains of Makeney in which the unnamed writer sought financial support on account of her being ill all winter of '... third day ague'.[19] Treatments for ague were a common feature of seventeenth- to nineteenth-century Derbyshire recipe books such as ones from Baslow, Eyam and Hopwell Hall.[17,19,20] It is notable that Makeney, Baslow and Eyam are in, or close to potential malarial areas within, the valley of the River Derwent. Across in Shropshire, an outbreak of ague in Bridgenorth, in 1784 is particularly well documented (Coley 1785). The early parish registers of Trentham in nearby Staffordshire indicate that ague was a common cause of death (Wrottesley 1906).

Wales does not appear to have escaped the ague, particularly in low-lying coastal areas. In north Wales the disease was prevalent in the flat areas around Rhuddlan, the Clwyd valley, the area between Porthmadog and Aberglaslyn, around Dolgellau, and on Anglesey (Sanders 1771, Walford 1818, Long and Porter 1849, Mason 1867, Ewart 1902). In old Flintshire, a late seventeenth-century letter to Sir John Trevor, concerning his land along the River Alun, seeks instruction on how to treat a destitute widow Roberts [of Pen yr allt Goch, Hoseley, near Gresford] and her seven children who had all been '... sick of a 3 [tertian] ague a long time'.[21] In south Wales ague appeared commonly around Fishguard, Carmathen, Aberavon and the parishes of Llandough and Leckwith in the Vale of Glamorgan (Lewis 1840, Ewart 1902). It is also reported occasionally from river valleys in central Wales, as in Radnorshire (Sanders 1771). Many of these references note the diminution or disappearance of the disease following land drainage.

Patterns of mortality in riverside parishes along the Severn estuary in Gloucestershire during the fourteenth century were probably attributable to ague (Franklin 1983). Isolated cases were reported from around Penzance (Forbes 1836) and around the mouth of the River Exe in Devon. Persons afflicted with ague are said to have sought a cure by visiting a nearby crossroad on five different occasions at the dead of night to bury an egg, symbolic of the ague they wished to shed (Harland 1858). Elsewhere in the West Country ague was prevalent in the Somerset Levels. For example, at a meeting of the West Somerset branch of the British Medical Society in 1882, the president noted that locally in low-lying areas ' ... ague has been much less frequent than formerly: for several years it has been gradually diminishing' (Anon 1882).

Ague is also known to have occurred in Ireland, with a report on public health in Dublin noting that a medical witness recounted that '... I remember people talking about being afflicted with ague in Dublin in the olden time' (Anon 1900b). An account of a visit to Ireland by Thomas Dineley Esq. during the reign of Charles II warns that 'English new come over here are incident to ... [among other diseases] agues' (Shirley 1856). A particularly bad outbreak of ague in Dublin in 1720 caused Dean Swift, author of *Gulliver's Travels*, to '... express his fears' about catching the disease (Womersley 2009).

It is to Scotland, however, that we must turn to find the closest parallels to Cumbria, both in topography and climate. Finlay (1978, 1980) has suggested that the recorded disease may be something other than vivax malaria but the evidence for true ague appears overwhelming. Comrie (1927), in his *History of Scottish Medicine*, wrote that '... Among the diseases of the seventeenth and eighteenth centuries, which those medical practitioners who happened to be available found themselves frequently called upon to treat, were smallpox and ague. Ague or malaria was a disease that caused much trouble in the seventeenth and eighteenth centuries'. The impact was particularly harshly felt among the poor (Graham 1899). Among early mentions is a report of c. 1680, in the Royal Society archives, written by the Duke of York, concerning the incidence of ague in Scotland.[35] In this he recorded having '... ye opportunity to enquire off a studious person who is one of ye chiefs of ye Scottish nobility ... about ye infrequency of agues in his Country'. He then proceeded briefly to mention specific cases. Ague was also listed among the complaints most frequently treated by an Aberdeen doctor in the late seventeenth-century, although his charges for treatment were well beyond the means of all but the wealthiest patients (Mitchell 1939). Forty years later, some of the first patients treated at the newly opened Edinburgh Royal Infirmary in 1729 were four cases of ague (Anon 1929) and the minister of the parish of Longforgan near Dundee, noted in the 1700s that '... ague was rather common in the low-lying districts' of the parish (Philip 1895).

Our understanding of the geographical reach of ague in Scotland, however, owes much to Prof. James Ritchie of Aberdeen University (Ritchie 1920, Anon 1932, Risse 2005). Ritchie, in a much neglected work, mapped ague in Scotland (fig. 4), primarily from accounts of the disease in each parish, submitted by parish ministers and published in Sinclair's *Statistical Account of Scotland* (Sinclair 1791-99). His map identified ague hot spots in the eastern Borders region across to Berwick on Tweed, in the Lothians and lower-lying areas of Fife, Tayside and Grampian (see also Carlisle 1813, Barbieri 1857, Day

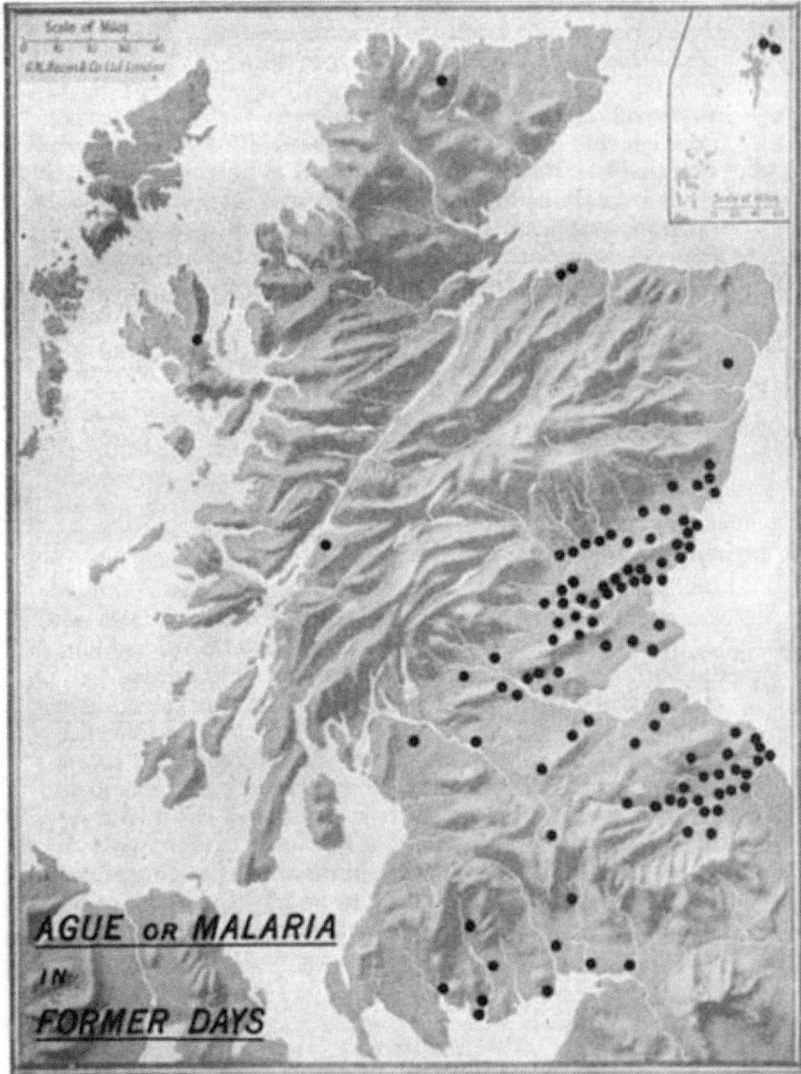

DISTRIBUTION OF AGUE OR MALARIA IN SCOTLAND IN THE 18th CENTURY.
Each dot indicates a parish where Ague was common.

Fig. 4. Map showing the historical extent of ague in Scotland. Reproduced from Professor James Ritchie's *The Influence of Man on Animal Life in Scotland* (1920).

1915, Paul 1922). Ague also occurred, most significantly for adjacent Cumbria, at scattered localities along the Solway in present-day Dumfries and Galloway, including the Wigtown parish of Kirkinner (Anon 1845a). MacKenzie (1841), in his *History of Galloway*, observed that '... The draining of marshes and mosses, the erection of more spacious and better ventilated houses ... the nutritious diet now used and the greater attention to cleanliness have banished several diseases – such as the ague – which prevailed to a painful degree'. Ague was also surprisingly reported sporadically from parishes as far north as Shetland and Orkney, although these could well be isolated imported cases (see also Anon 1845a). It is notable that many of the Scottish records related to inland sites, such as Moffat and Kelso, far removed from the coastal marshes (Anon 1845a).

Old medical reports further support these observations. The Aberdeen physician, Patrick Chalmers, practising at the turn of the seventeenth century, listed ague as one of the most frequent diseases in old Aberdeenshire (Comrie 1927). The surviving records of Kelso Dispensary (1777-1785) in the Borders are particularly illuminating. For example the average case-load, including those who travelled for treatment from neighbouring parishes, averaged around 600 cases of ague per annum during this period (Wilson 1841, Creighton 1894). An earlier letter, dated 1724, from Dr Abernethy of Kelso to a Mr Hood regarding his ague suggests that the disease was already present in the area.[32] Like elsewhere, ague went into decline in Scotland from the end of the eighteenth century onwards (Comrie 1927). At the meeting of the National Association for the Promotion of Social Science in 1863 Dr Christison declared that '... there is [now] no ague in Scotland' (Anon 1863a, Christison 1863). The statistics, however, tell otherwise. Indeed in 1843 Dr William Farr noted that amongst the poor '... influenza and ague were growing more fatal every year' (Hodgkinson 1967). This most probably referred to its virulence in the individual rather than to its more widespread nature. Scottish death statistics of the 1850s and 1860s also record a small number of deaths from ague. For example in 1857, 1861 and 1867 the number of deaths was three, six and one respectively (Anon 1862-1869). As late as 1902 requests for Poor Law relief on account of ague were still being met by the parish of Glasgow (Anon 1904).

The ague in Cumbria

Ague was most prevalent in Cumbria before systematic recording of disease statistics was initiated. Indeed the working poor probably suffered the disease as part of their burden and did not seek help, except as a very last resort. As a result incidence of the disease probably remains largely unrecorded, except in folk memory. New farm tenants in malarial areas, for example, are said to have accepted a '... seasoning fever' as part of their lot (Garnett 1912).

Several publications record the once widespread and common occurrence of ague in Cumbria generally. An address to the Penrith District Agricultural Society in 1840 observed that '...throughout the whole of Cumberland, owing to draining and judicious planting, ... The tertian and other agues with which they were so familiar when boys were now scarcely heard of' (Anon 1840). Among general guides, Mannex's (1849) *History of Westmorland*, for example, noted that '... agues were then remarkably prevalent in Spring'. Dickinson (1875) in his *Cumbriana* remarked that '... Previous to the draining period, the ague had been a prevalent disease in the neighbourhood of moist localities.' Similarly, Daniel Scott (1899) in his *Bygone Cumberland and Westmorland*, unaware of Ross's recently published work on mosquito vectors, observed that a '... meagre diet was probably the cause of the agues, which were once very common, especially in the country districts'. Hutchinson (1794) in his *History of Cumbria* specifically identified Eskdale and the parish of Ponsonby, north of Gosforth, as '... strangers to the ague', observations suggesting that they were exceptions worthy of note. Harriet Martineau (1854, 1855) in her separate guides to Windermere and to the English Lakes expressed the general concern about ague by observing that the water mill at Newby Bridge had ceased to function and called for its replacement by steam pumps to prevent the formation of swamps that would lead to the return of ague and other diseases.

Ague in the rural areas

Ague was widespread throughout the old counties of Westmorland and Cumberland and in Lancashire North of the Sands (fig.5). It was, as described below for various localities, particularly prevalent in low-lying marshy areas fringing Morecambe Bay but it is recorded from several places within the central Lake District and in low-lying districts around Carlisle and Whitehaven. It is interesting that the coastal fringe has a slightly warmer climate, more akin to that of southern England, than the remainder of Cumbria, making it more susceptible to successful breeding by some species of mosquito vector.

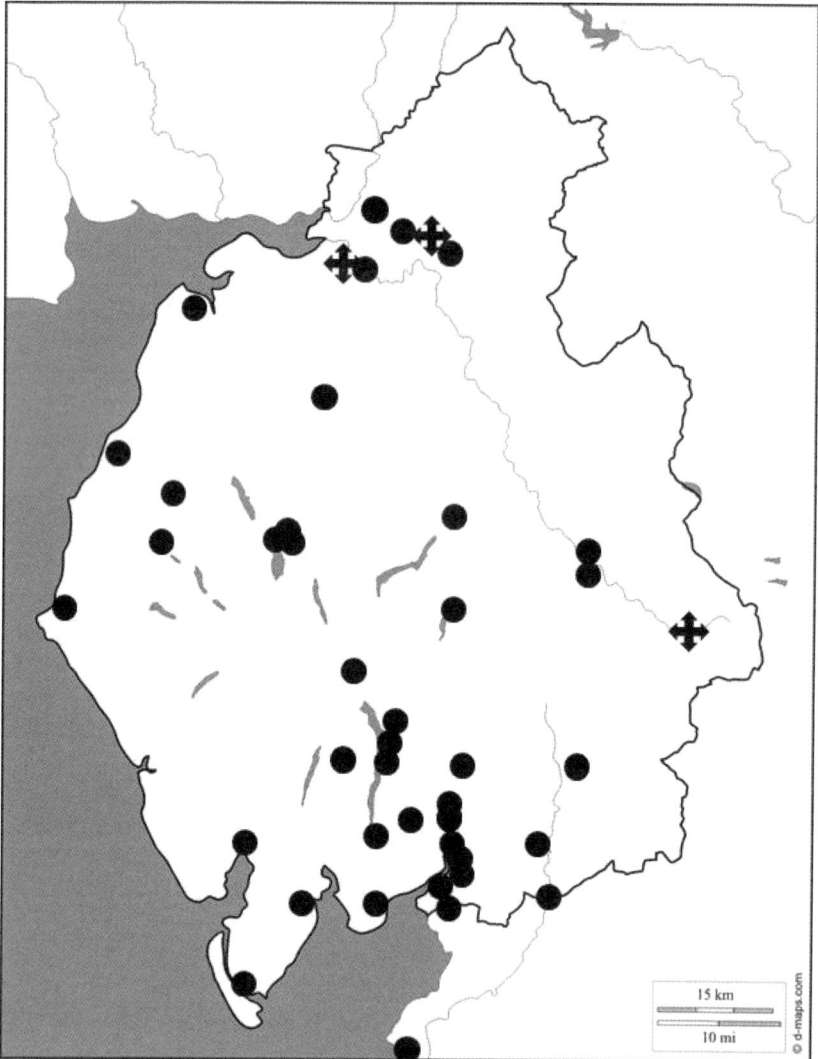

Fig. 5. Map of ague in Cumbria in the seventeenth to nineteenth century. Black circles indicate places for which there is documentary evidence for the presence of ague. The four-way arrow symbols indicate places where the record refers to cases in which a person with ague had recently visited the malarial areas of south-east England.

16

Heversham

The autobiography of Richard Stout of Lancaster notes that '... in 1678 my father took me to the schoole in Hearsom [Heversham] in Westmorland ... but about the 8th month that year I was seized with a third day ague which continued all that winter' (Anon 1850, Marshall 1967). A report of a lecture by Mr Ellison in the *Kendal Mercury* for 1848 records that 'Forty years ago, before the mosses in Heversham parish were enclosed, the doctors used to have 12 to 14 cases of ague continually under their care' (Anon 1848).

Milnthorpe

An inquest into the death of an un-named man in Milnthorpe workhouse in 1867 reported that previously he '...complained of being cold and shivering and said that he had had the ague and that he was afraid that he was going to have it again' (Anon 1867b). The jury returned a verdict of '... Died by the Visitation of God'!

Storth

An S. Postlethwaite of Beetham, in a letter dated 11 June 1745, describes how Turlington's Balsam of Life was used to treat patients with ague and intermittent fever in Storth. The letter was published, as a testimonial, in a pamphlet extolling the virtue of the balsam and seeking patent protection for its formulation (Anon 1750) (fig. 6). The same Storth testimonials appeared, earlier, in an advertisement for Turlington's Balsam in *The Penny London Post* (Anon 1748).

By Virtue of the King's Patent

G II R

TURLINGTON's Balsam of Life

Is Prepared and Sold by the PATENTEE, in *Lombard-Street, London* :

(Price 3s. 6d. the Bottle.)

The Efficacy and Virtues of which Incomparable Medicine are exemplified by an Account of some of the Cures perform'd thereby, in this Book briefly mention'd.

Fig. 6. 1745 pamphlet for Turlington's Balsam.

Drybeck

William Abram in 1729 petitioned Westmorland Quarter Sessions for relief as he was unable to maintain himself because of ague.[13] This was one of the few cases where relief was not granted.

The Yealands

Although the Yealands are not strictly part of Cumbria the adjacent mosslands formed a continuous system of poorly-drained marshland. There is a tradition in the area that '... plagues and agues do not come where peat is burnt' (Ford and Fuller-Maitland 1931, Lofthouse 1953). This observation suggests that ague was well known. It is ironic in that peat smoke is likely to deter mosquitoes but that digging the peat is, in the first place, likely to expose the gatherer to mosquito bites.

Levens Hall

Ann Bagot, in her account of Guillaume Beaumont, head gardener at Levens Hall, records that in 1721 '... Beaumont has his spring indisposition but recovers' and the following year she notes that '... Beaumont is suffering from fits of ague every day' (Bagot 1975). It appears that Beaumont was not averse to the liberal use of alcohol to relieve his condition.

Lyth

In what appears to be an account of the same meeting addressed by Mr Ellison (see under Heversham), the *Westmorland Gazette* reported a somewhat different version of events (Anon 1848). It records that

> ... after the drainage was accomplished on the mosses the fogs all disappeared. He [Mr Ellison] recollected that at the time the late lamented Dr. Tatham used to have regularly from twelve to fifteen patients in Lyth ill of the ague during the season and after the [enclosure] acts of parliament he used to say – Hang these acts of parliament, they are taking away our trade.

The Kendal land agent and surveyor, Crayston Webster, writing in 1868, observed that '... There are still remaining patches of the ancient mosses, around the margins of which, as for many ages past, peats are got by native farmers and by the villagers of Brigsteer and Beathwaite Green [now Levens] ... before this drainage ague was a common complaint' (Webster 1868).

Underbarrow

At a public meeting on the sanitary condition of Kendal a long-standing resident, Mr. Noble, recalled that 'Underbarrow, which when he first commenced his career, was the seat of ague, was now thoroughly drained' (Anon 1845c). A Thomas Harrison of Underbarrow was called before the Archdeacon's correction court in 1765 for '... not attending chapel.' He claimed he was '... indisposed with an ague'. [23]

Kirkby Lonsdale area

The one-time MP for Westmorland, Thomas Fenwick Esq of Burrow Hall, south of Kirkby Lonsdale (and just in Lancashire), received a letter from a Mr Hurd dated 1783 in which the latter informed him that the price of red Peruvian bark was 6s and pale 5s per pound (Holt 2011). No order to purchase bark is recorded but Fenwick was clearly interested in its use as he later that year noted that he '... Took 3 drams of bark for J. Davis's son in an ague'. In 1788 he noted that '... James Sisson came [to Burrow Hall] but he was seized with the ague which obliged him to go home' (Holt 2011).

Appleby area

The surgeon William Bayers in his *Medico-topographical Sketches of Appleby* reveals that '... I have been informed by very intelligent old people of my native dale, that in their younger days, ague was very common, that they themselves were frequently attacked by it' (Bayers 1824). He goes on to point out that '...The almost entire extinctions of agues in the northern parts ... has been attributed to the draining of wet and marshy lands' but then notes that '... in my native dale there never have been any marshes and the surface-draining made use of on the hills and pasture lands, can do nothing more than contract the trifling moisture of extensive surface into narrower bounds'. Having pointed out that Appleby was not a prime environment for ague to flourish, he then expresses some mystification as to why agues disappeared from his area, suggesting improved food and clothing and a '... difference of temperature'.

Witherslack

Hodgson (1937) in his *Glimpses of Witherslack* observed that '... the lack of green vegetables, together with the low lying situation of many of the homes, caused inflammatory diseases, and ague was very common'. A good specific example is found in the diary of the Rev. Thomas Brockbank for 1709, who recorded that '... John at Witherslack has been severely handled with an ague' (Trappes Lomax 1930). From 1779 to 1800 ten people died within Witherslack parish of fevers that were not attributable to typhoid, typhus, cholera, influenza or plague (Jones 1971).

Cartmel

James Stockdale (1872) in his *Annales Caermolenses* observed that

> ... amongst many advantages attendant on the enclosure of the Cartmel commons is enumerated the entire expulsion thereby from the parish of Cartmel of that very plaguy complaint the ague. Often, have I heard my late father and other old persons say that previous to the enclosure of the commons in 1796, the ague was one of the most common complaints'.

He goes on to add that before enclosure '... in almost every part of Cartmel parish there were extensive morasses, swamps, pits, ponds, marshes, stagnant sheets of water, obstructed streams, and much undrained, or at any rate ineffectually drained, land' (see also Taylor 1955). A more detailed account of the drainage is given in the *Victoria County History of Lancashire* (Farrar and Brownbill 1914). It records that

> under the [Inclosure] Act some 8,000 acres of common land were dealt with ... deep drains were cut through the mosses and low lying lands and a long line of embankment was constructed to protect the marsh lands of Wyke, Bank Moor and Winder Moor from encroachment by the sea. A result not anticipated was the banishment of the ague.

A more personal account of ague in the village is included in the diary and letters of the Rev. Thomas Brockbank, who resided there from 1706 until his death. He recorded several episodes of ague within his family. A typical entry is that in a letter of 9 April 1707 in which he wrote 'Let sister know her son T has been somewhat hardly used with ye ague, sometimes shaking every day, sometimes every 2d day: but at least he has shaked it off' (Trappes-Lomax 1930).

Memories of the ague clearly persisted, as a report on a new heating system in Cartmel church from 1867 noted that '... one may worship in winter as well as in summer without the risk of a violent ague and serious after consequences' (Anon 1867a).

Tottlebank and Furness

Dibdin (1802), in his *Observations on a Tour through England and Scotland* recorded a conversation with a Keswick boatman who recalled that while living in Furness fifteen years previously '... he had been much troubled by the ague'. The records of the 'Church of Christ in Broughton Ffurnessfells and Cartmel' (Tottlebank) recount that a '... Mr Sedgefield came with his family to us about August 30 1724. But it pleasing the Lord to afflict him and wife with ague ...' (Channing 1985).

Salthouse (now part of Barrow)

The inhabitants of the seaside village of Salthouse, in the area that now lies just north of Barrow docks, were noted to have '... suffered badly from the ague in the eighteenth century...' (Marshall 1958). James Kendall of Hallbeck, describing Salthouse in 1760, reported that '... interspersed among the farm buildings were numerous ponds and mire plants', which did not add to the wholesomeness of the place, and it was no wonder that the inhabitants were liable to severe attacks of ague and other distressing complaints' (Kendall 1948). Women suffered particularly badly from ague, with a Mary Brockbank enduring repeated violent attacks. It is recorded that the last case, following improved drainage, was a Dorothy Kendall who died in 1821 (Kendall 1948).

Hawkshead

An account in the *Earlier Registers and Parish Accounts at Hawkshead*, dating from 1784, records the cost of brandy and ale, paid to a parishioner Sarah Usher '... to stop the ague' (Allen 1878). A later essay published in the *Westmorland Gazette* of 1856 entitled 'In Memory of Esthwaite Lake' extolled the virtue of drainage and talked of '... our forefathers reclining in their elbow-chairs shaking with ague ... as the effects of a life spent in swamp, mud and mist' (Anon 1856).

Calgarth and Windermere

A letter from Robert Philipson at Calgarth, north of Windermere, to Daniel Fleming in 1670, lamented that 'My wife hath been very sick this week almost, and I fear 't will prove an ague' (Fahy 1964). An early nineteenth-century travel guide, published in *Blackwood's Edinburgh Magazine* suggested visiting Belle Isle in Windermere. It issued a warning, however, to guard against marsh fever as the island had formerly been quite marshy and the shoreline much better vegetated (Anon 1826).

Troutbeck

Baines (1829), in his *Companion to the Lakes*, observed of Troutbeck that '... formerly rheumatism and ague were very prevalent in these parts: I believe that they are less so now'. The Browne family of Townend, with its longstanding residence at Troutbeck was the source, as noted elsewhere, of collected charms against the ague (Scott 1904). Furthermore, George Browne noted in a letter dated 1719 that 'I have been much indisposed since my last [letter] in an ague and Feavour, but, thank God am well recovered' (Scott 1904).

Rydal

William Fleming, in an undated letter from Rydal Hall between 1650 and 1680, writes that '... wee are all very well onely Tibb [short for Isabella] is troubled with a fit of an ague' (Magrath 1904). Another later missive to Fleming, from Thomas Dixon of Oxford mentions one of Fleming's sons contracting ague in Rydal (Magrath 1904, 1913). Yet another letter from Rydal dated 1692, to the then MP for Westmorland Sir Christopher Musgrave at Edenhall, near Langwathby, suggests that there was much ague about. He wrote that '... Many in this country have had the ague and three of my sons [he had 15 children] have had 3 or 4 fits apiece, and then gave over. I hope my cousin Dorothy and George will do the like'. He then proceeds to recommend treatment with Carduus Benedictus possets, even though a further scrap of paper in the Fleming family papers entitled 'For an ague' provides an alternative treatment.[11,12] Further details of both treatments are given later in this book under *Local folk remedies and doubtful cures*.

Cockermouth

The evidence for ague here is less strong but an article of 1860 on sanitary reform in the town draws attention to a 1846 government report stating that '... the decaying matters of marshes give rise to agues, dysenteries and fevers'. It goes on to imply that failure to observe the sanitary recommendations of that report with respect to the town's rivers, following the long hot summer of 1859, led to the occurrence of these diseases (Anon 1860).

Underwood (3 km NNW of Loweswater)

Isaac Fletcher kept a diary at Underwood from 1756 to 1781. In it he records several instances of ague, both in himself and among associates. An entry in 1778, for example, describes a typical ague fit: '... Very unwell. Got a severe fitt of the ague upon me. Shaked and had very hot fitts and cold'. In 1774, a doctor was called to treat 'Nanny' who was ill with an intermittent fever (Winchester 1994).

Keswick district

A report into the sanitary condition of Keswick, when discussing typhoid and other diseases, remarked that '... the maladies being alluded to are quite [as] capable of being expelled from the valley as ague, which by a better system of drainage, has been entirely removed during the last half century (Anon 1852c). Similarly, a nineteenth-century *Handbook for the Use of Visitors* talks of '... Agues and fevers, of a character happily now unknown, arising from the vicinage of extensive swamps and undrained marshlands, periodically visited and carried off a portion of the inhabitants' (Anon 1852b). In a medical paper that examined whether there existed an incompatibility between infections of ague and consumption a Dr. Southey remarked that '... in the Vale of Keswick, in Cumberland, agues were formerly very common, but have nearly disappeared' (Boudin et al. 1849). The name Southey surfaced again in the context of Keswick and ague when the poet Robert Southey recorded the memory of an aged lady friend who recalled that 'Ague was so prevalent in the Vale of Keswick, that a servant maid who came only from a few miles' distance, had to make up her mind to a '... six weeks shake' (Coleridge 1851). However, Southey subsequently noted that '... ague is beginning to reappear, which had scarcely been heard of during the last generation' (Southey 1850). It seems that as late as 1841 the village of Braithwaite was '... the only place hereabouts remarkable for fevers' (Southey 1850). Even so, while staying in Keswick in 1880, General William Booth, the founder of the Salvation Army, wrote that '... I have been very poorly since we came, my old enemy, the slow, ague fever, having been on me for a fortnight' (Begbie 1926). It is notable that in the late nineteenth century Cumberland was in the top eight English counties for registered deaths from ague and intermittent fever (Davidson 1892). In these pestilential circumstances it is not surprising that the church book of Keswick Congregational Church in the late 1700s contained 'a cure for the ague' (see fig. 12. p.41).[1]

Solway marshes

Ewart et al. (1902), in a medical paper on the climate of Great Britain, recorded the past occurrence of just '... occasional cases [of ague]'.

Sebergham

Eleanora Hewett petitioned Cumberland Quarter Sessions for relief in 1728 on account of her husband dying seven weeks previously '... after a long Sickness of ten weeks in an ague and fever'. [3]

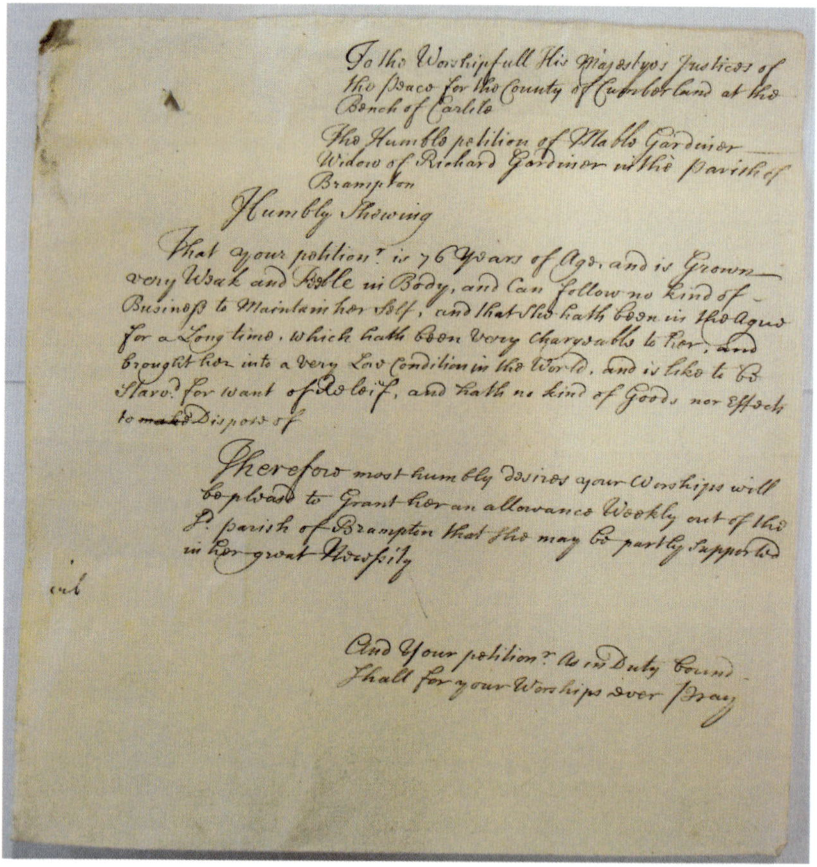

To the Worshipfull His Majestyes Justices of the Peace for the County of Cumberland at the Bench of Carlile

The Humble petition of Mable Gardiner Widow of Richard Gardiner in the parish of Brampton

Humbly Shewing

That your petition.r is 76 Years of Age, and is Grown very Weak and Feeble in Body, and Can follow no kind of Business to Maintain her Self, and that She hath been in the Ague for a Long time, which hath been very Chargeable to her, and brought her into a very Low Condition in the World, and is like to be Starv.d for want of Releif, and hath no kind of Goods nor Effects to ~~make~~ Dispose of

Therefore most humbly desires your Worships will be pleased to Grant her an allowance Weekly out of the S.d parish of Brampton that she may be partly Supported in her great Necessity

And Your petition.r As in Duty bound Shall for your Worships ever Pray

Fig. 7. Petition of Mabel Gardiner of Brampton parish, near Carlisle, recorded at Cumberland Quarter Sessions in 1736, for financial support on account of being feeble and long-troubled by ague (Courtesy of Cumbria Archives, Carlisle).

Brampton

There are two petitions for relief to Cumberland Quarter Sessions involving cases of ague in the village. Isabell Hudless, a widow of Cumcatch Mill, pleaded in 1730 that she had the '... ague and other illnesses'. Mabel Gardiner, a widow, implored in 1736 that she was '... long troubled by ague' (fig.7). The former supplicant possibly acquired her infection at Alston Moor. It is indicative of the serious debilitating effect of ague and the inability of the petitioner to support themselves or their family, that in almost all cases such requests for financial or other assistance were granted.[4,7]

Kirklinton

In 1738 a Jane Addison petitioned twice for relief at Cumberland Quarter Sessions having '... been in the Ague Ever since Martinmas day last'.[8,9] It appears she contracted ague while working in the south.

Farlam

A petition to Cumberland Quarter Sessions in 1733 by Edward Hetheringon, the father of three dependent children, stated that he has '... had an Ague or Intermittent Fever these last several months and is now too weak to work'.[6]

Irthington

A similar petition in 1732 from Mary Reay of Irdington (= Irthington), an elderly widow, was granted as she was very sickly ' ... and is now in the Ague'[5] (fig.8).

Mardale

Elizabeth Lynn Linton (1864), in her book *The Lake Country*, describes a cottage and farmstead in the hamlet of Measands, now submerged below Haweswater. She recounts '... the children playing with fever and ague at its side'.

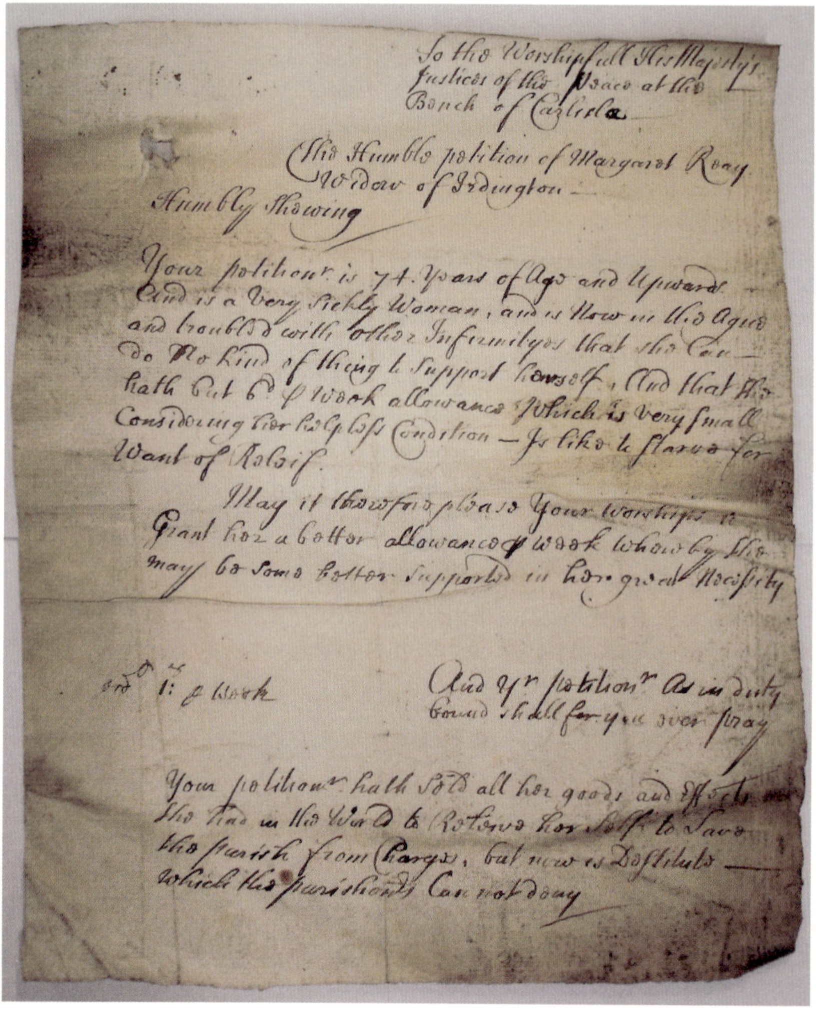

To the Worshipfull His Majesty's Justices of the Peace at the Bench of Carlisle

The Humble petition of Margaret Reay Widow of Irdington

Humbly Shewing

Your petition^r is 74 Years of Age and Upwards And is a Very Sickly Woman, and is Now in the Ague and troubled with other Infirmityes that she Can do No kind of thing to Support herself, And that she hath but 6^d ℘ Week allowance Which is very Small Considering her helpless Condition — Is like to starve for Want of Releif.

May it therefore please Your Worships to Grant her a better allowance ℘ Week whereby She may be some better Supported in her great Necessity

ord 1^s ℘ Week

And Y^r petition^r As in duty bound shall for you ever pray

Your petition^r hath Sold all her goods and Effects She had in the World to Releive her Self to Save the parish from Charges, but now is Destitute — which the parishoners Can not deny

Fig. 8. Petition of Margaret Reay of Irthington recorded at Cumberland Quarter Sessions in 1732 for financial support on account of her incapacity to support herself through the effects of ague (Courtesy of Cumbria Archives, Carlisle).

Ague in the main towns

Kendal

Probably the most complete record of ague in Cumbria is for Kendal where its prevalence is well documented in general accounts of the town. Hodgson (1810) in his *Topographical Historical and Descriptive Delineations of Westmorland* noted that '... the houses being generally built in low situations, and foot or two within the ground, caused agues to be prevalent here in the spring'. Later, Nicholson (1832), in his *Annals of Kendal*, observed that '... Agues and scrofulous disorders abounded here half a century ago'. Curwen in his account of *Kirkbie-Kendall* (1900) recounted that '... the land by the riverside ... was far too swampy to permit of the town's main road ...passing along it. So that those who passed to and fro, being mindful of the ague, chose the higher and harder ground to the west.' A study of the *Topographical Pathology of Kendal* by Proudfoot also recorded that '... On the west of Stricklandgate, or between this part of the town and the hill, there is an unoccupied space, which was formerly a morass or swamp .... This marsh was formerly considered the parent of intermittent fevers. Since the draining, these have entirely disappeared' (Proudfoot 1822, reproduced in Ashcroft 2001). Boott (1834) in his *Memoir of John Armstrong M.D.* suggested more generally that the lower reaches of the Kent Valley down to the sea might be a further source of the infection. A later account (Anon 1849) qualified Proudfoot's conclusions by misquoting him and talking about *limited* drainage and only a *partial* disappearance of intermittent fever. A further discrepancy mistakenly placed the swamp north-east of the town and named it Maude's Meadow. Despite much discussion work fully to drain Maude's Meadow did not commence until 1864 (Anon 1853a, 1864a). Nevertheless, Proudfoot listed the annual number of cases of intermittent fever (ague) dealt with by Kendal Dispensary between 1795 and 1821, a period when cases were declining. These totalled 118, with a maximum of 19 in 1809 (Proudfoot 1822, Nuttall et al. 1901).

The desperate human straits that ague left in its wake are illustrated by one townsperson, Joseph Weber, who deliberately begged at Kendal Police Office to get himself arrested with the specific purpose of obtaining medical advice and shelter (Anon 1843a). His wish was granted and he was willingly committed for 14 days.

The general sanitation conditions in Kendal were the subject of much subsequent discussion in local newspapers, particularly the stagnant drains and their outlets into the River Kent as a source of cholera and typhoid as well as malaria. In 1846 a public meeting was convened to press for improved sanitation involving an enhanced supply of clean water for drinking and to keep the drains, 'the principal hotbeds of malaria', well flushed out (Anon1846). As late as 1865 the vicar of Kendal took Alderman Wilson to show him 'the source of the fever' where a foul drain emptied into a dry bed of the River Kent below Nether Bridge. Occasional cases described unhelpfully as 'simple continued fever', possibly ague, continued up until 1873 (Page 1875).

Ulverston

Whitley (1864) cites a Dr Dickinson of Ulverston who had not come across any cases of ague in 30 years' of practice but who recounted hearing from others that intermittent fevers had been common in the area at the beginning of the [nineteenth] century (see also Nuttall et al. 1901).

Whitehaven

William Brownrigg, the Whitehaven physician, records that '... During this Epidemical Season [early 1731] Agues were stirring' (Brownrigg 1993). He did not specifically mention Peruvian bark as a remedy (see later) but was aware of its existence and included it in his prescription for convulsive coughing. The parish records for Holy Trinity Church 1751-1780 list 'fever' as a major cause of mortality but ague was not separated from other fever-producing diseases (Ward 1998). It is known, however, that the vicar at that time, Thomas Sewel, self-administered Peruvian bark and '... had recourse to it so often that he used to eat it greedily when at his books' (Brownrigg 1993,Ward 1998). Dr. Joshua Dixon regularly recorded multiple cases of 'intermittent fever' in his reports of the Whitehaven Dispensary between 1783 and 1823 (Dixon 1783-1823[16]). These are now thought, by a present-day Whitehaven doctor, to be cases of ague (Sydney 2009). Other sporadic cases occurred until the 1860s with the Whitehaven Board of Guardians granting financial relief to Thomas Ellwood as he was '... suffering from ague and rheumatism'(Anon 1863b, 1865). The following year one death was reported from intermittent fever in the Union Workhouse, following ten weeks of debility (Anon 1866).

William Dickinson (1852), in his treatise *On the Farming of*

Cumberland, noted significantly that

> Fifty years ago a great part of the now fertile meadows in the valley
> extending from Whitehaven to St. Bees were peat mosses, full of
> holes from whence peat had been dug. They were then a fruitful
> source of fever and ague: the late Dr. Joshua Dixon attributed the
> greater part of the sanitary improvement of Whitehaven since that
> period to the effective drainage of these meadows by Mr. Benn,
> the agent to the late Earl of Lonsdale.

Maryport

A report into the sanitary state of the town in 1864 highlighted how
diseases spread from Whitehaven and recorded that 'we are now
visited by a low intermittent fever' (Anon 1864b).

Carlisle

An inquest into the death of a William Barnes in Carlisle Gaol
in 1763 recorded that he '... died of the ague having suffered
8 or 9 weeks'.[10] Hutchinson (1794) in his *History of the County of
Cumberland* noted an epidemic of a relapsing fever within the city in
1785. The annual *Bills of Mortality in Carlisle* record sporadic deaths
from ague and list the number of people receiving treatment at
Carlisle Dispensary, following its foundation in 1782. The surviving
records from the eighteenth century are, however, incomplete and
provide only a fragmentary glimpse of the disease, with the number
of people treated for ague varying from 20+ in 1783 and 1784 to
eight and four respectively in 1786 and 1787 (Heysham 1779-1789,
Lonsdale 1870). The disease continued well until the nineteenth
century, with seven cases cured by Peruvian bark (and arsenic!!) at
the Carlisle Dispensary in the spring of 1821 (Anon 1821). A letter,
dated 1830, from a Miss Anne Lacy, among the Huddleston family
correspondence, expressed concern that Ellen Carlyle of Carlisle was
'... reduced to a skeleton by ague'.[2] Miss Ellen Carlyle, then a well-
known political activist and friend of Lord Wallace, chronicled her
own illness in letters to friends dated April to June 1830.[30] In one she
apologised that '... The wretchedness of my ague has prevented my
answering your letter'.

A later meeting to discuss improvements to public health in Carlisle
in 1847 concluded that '... The spirits of our forefathers taunt us
with neglect – they point to our immunity from plague, from ague
and other scourges, as a legacy they have left us'. This was essentially

a plea to deal with current diseases as they had dealt with ague in the past (Anon 1847). However, in the spring of 1854 one of the prevailing diseases in Carlisle, particularly amongst children, was intermittent fever (Anon 1854). In 1859 three cases of intermittent fever were recorded at Carlisle Dispensary (Whitley 1864) and reports of such fevers persisted into the 1860s. The Carlisle Distress Fund Committee in 1862 granted financial relief to the Berry family whose eldest girl '... was lying ill of intermittent fever' (Anon 1862a).

Penrith

A study of marital fertility at Penrith 1557-1812 suggested that malnutrition made the population less able 'to resist diseases such as ague' and that this resulted in low rates of fertility (Scott and Duncan 1996).

Importation of malaria into Cumbria and the north

People travelled around the country, often for seasonal agricultural employment, and in so doing transferred malaria and other diseases between localities (Eccles 1989). The best documented examples are where people have moved temporarily into a known malaria area, often in south-east England, and then returned and become incapacitated, making them unfit to travel or work and thus requiring financial relief. For example, Westmorland Quarter Sessions in 1756 granted a '... horse pass' to Alexander Cowen from Kirkandrews-on Eden, who spent three months at the corn harvest in the Lincolnshire fen country. On his return he got as far as Brough before becoming too weak with ague to travel and he thus required assistance to reach home.[14] Similarly, in 1766 John Cairns of Carlisle spent seven weeks at the harvest in Cambridgeshire and Lincolnshire, contracted ague, became sickly and was apprehended in Brough. He was granted a horse pass to assist him to reach home (fig. 9) (Gowling 2011[15]). The *Bills of Mortality for Carlisle* in 1780 included one death from '... ague contracted in the South' (Heysham 1781).

Comparable cases occurred in the 1800s. An outbreak of ague amongst workmen on the Carlisle Canal in 1821 was attributed to some of the crew having picked up their infection in Lincolnshire (Anon 1821). A man with ague, appearing before Westmorland Michaelmas Sessions in 1852, had previously '... been a resident

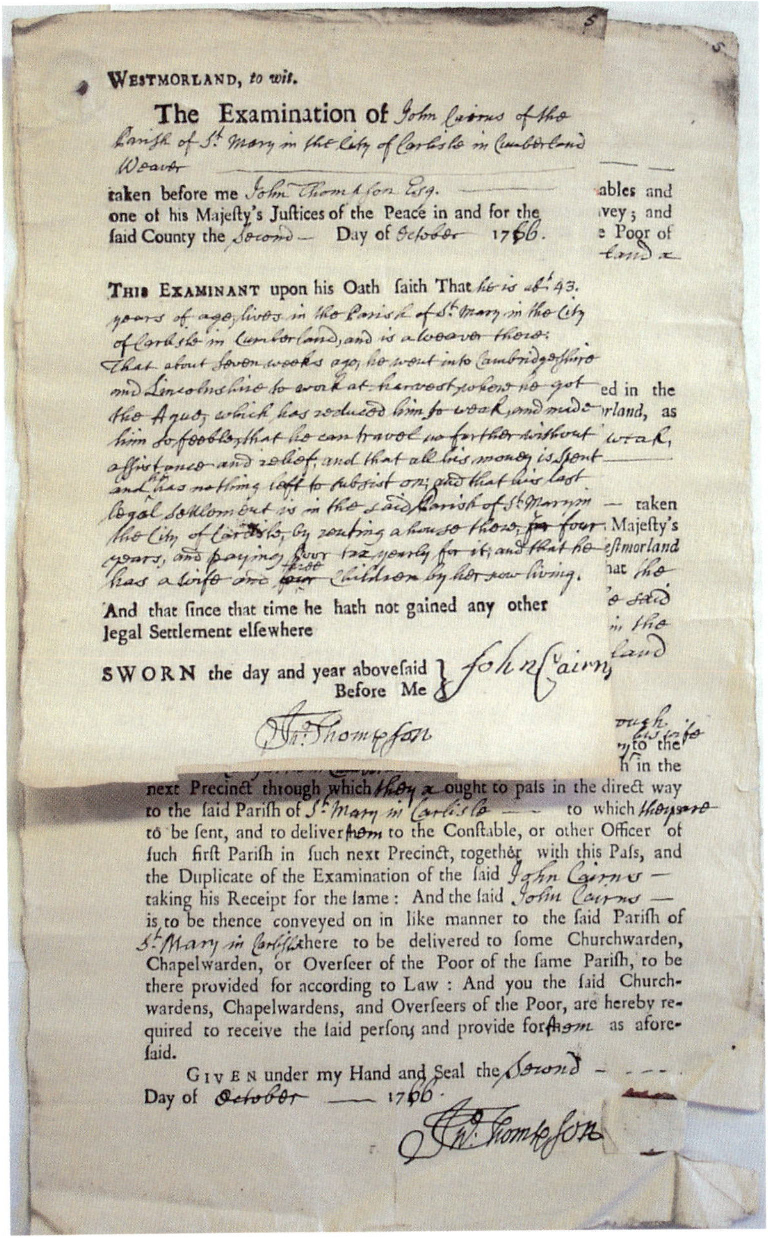

WESTMORLAND, *to wit.*

The Examination of John Cairns of the Parish of St. Mary in the City of Carlisle in Cumberland Weaver

taken before me John Thompson Esq. one of his Majesty's Justices of the Peace in and for the said County the Second Day of October 1766.

THIS EXAMINANT upon his Oath saith That he is abt. 43. years of age, lives in the Parish of St. Mary in the City of Carlisle in Cumberland, and is a weaver there: That about seven weeks ago, he went into Cambridgeshire and Lincolnshire to work at harvest, where he got the Ague, which has reduced him so weak, and made him so feeble, that he can travel no further without assistance and relief, and that all his money is spent and he has nothing left to subsist on; and that his last legal settlement is in the said Parish of St. Mary in the City of Carlisle, by renting a house there, for four years, and paying four pounds yearly for it; and that he has a wife and first Children by her now living.

And that since that time he hath not gained any other legal Settlement elsewhere

SWORN the day and year abovesaid Before Me } John Cairns

Jn. Thompson

next Precinct through which they ought to pass in the direct way to the said Parish of St. Mary in Carlisle to which they are to be sent, and to deliver them to the Constable, or other Officer of such first Parish in such next Precinct, together with this Pass, and the Duplicate of the Examination of the said John Cairns taking his Receipt for the same: And the said John Cairns is to be thence conveyed on in like manner to the said Parish of St. Mary in Carlisle there to be delivered to some Churchwarden, Chapelwarden, or Overseer of the Poor of the same Parish, to be there provided for according to Law: And you the said Churchwardens, Chapelwardens, and Overseers of the Poor, are hereby required to receive the said persons and provide for them as aforesaid.

GIVEN under my Hand and Seal the Second Day of October 1766.

Jn. Thompson

Fig. 9. Horse pass issued in 1766 at Appleby Quarter Sessions for John Cairns, incapacitated with ague (Courtesy of Cumbria Archives, Kendal).

amongst the fens in Lincolnshire where he had been exposed to the exciting cause of the disease [ague]' (Anon 1852d). A case in the Morpeth Deanery, Northumberland, where the disease spread rapidly throughout the family of a worker returning from Lincolnshire, also indicates that potential carrier mosquitoes must have already been present in the area (Hodgson 1825). Ague may have also travelled in the opposite direction. The Quaker William Gibson, following a visit to Lancashire, is recorded as being '... seized by an ague and fever at Coventry' (Gough 1789).

During and just after World War 1 returning troops reintroduced *P. vivax* malaria into Britain where it became established in the mosquito population of England, especially along the south and south-east coasts. Local people contracted the disease, with 330 cases recorded in one year (Shute 1945). Even today, malaria is continually imported into the UK from abroad and there are still odd incidences of people living around airports contracting the disease, although this is usually the more deadly *P. falciparum* (Whitfield et al. 1984). Data for England in 2013 and 2014 show 1412 and 1415 cases of imported malaria annually, of which around 25% were *P. vivax* (Anon 2015, Gill 2015). Cases reported to Cumbria and Lancashire Public Health England Centre alone numbered 24 and 14 and were significantly greater in the north-west than elsewhere in England. North-West England has a significantly higher proportion of its population with ancestral links to areas of Asia where *P. vivax* is still endemic (Gill 2015).

The effects of ague on rural populations and agricultural production

Ague was clearly a debilitating disease that prevented people from carrying out their normal day-to-day activities and at worst resulted in death. It almost certainly had a disproportionate impact on the mortality rate of the rural poor (Healey 2008). However, accounts describing directly the effects on whole rural populations in northern areas where the disease was common are scarce. Skirving (1873), quoting from two earlier sources (including Grierson 1839), provides a particularly poignant exception, contrasting the health of the population of the Berwickshire and east Lothian area with that of Northumberland, which was relatively free of ague. He noted that in the former area '... At that period, regularly in the spring, in every hamlet and village the ague made its appearance in almost every family ... The consequences were that the poor were miserably fed, poorly clad, feeble and particularly liable to sickness'. He observed that in Northumberland the people were '... lusty fellows, fresh complexioned, cleanly and well clothed; but on crossing the border we generally find them lank, lean, hard featured, sallow, soiled and shabby ... the cattle are much the same as their drivers – meagre, stunted and ill equipt'. This raises the additional possibility that in ague areas mosquitoes may also have taken a toll on the condition of cattle as well as the human population.

Detailed descriptions of the effect of ague on individual families are similarly hard to find and usually emerge briefly when application is made for financial relief. It is clear that ague often affected whole families simultaneously and where the working adults were incapacitated it produced severe poverty. Widow Roberts in Flintshire, mentioned earlier, is a prime example.[21] She had seven children, as well as herself, affected by a tertian ague at the same time. In her successful petition for relief to Cumberland Quarter Session in 1738, Jane Addison of Kirklinton, a recent widow, was described in poverty as follows:[8]

> At the death of her husband she was left with 2 small children, which she has endeavoured by hard labour to bring up and was in the south the last summer working for her bread and came home with the ague that has continued ever since ... Everyday trembling and can do nothing for herself or her poor children nor has she any goods or effects but all was sold to pay the debts.

It goes on to describe how she spent the previous winter unable to work and had to sell all her belongings and became reliant on kindly parishioners to avoid starvation.

Old parish registers have been widely used to examine historic patterns of births, marriages, and particularly deaths, in rural populations. Unfortunately, most parish registers in Cumbria and Lancashire do not record the cause of death but, nevertheless, attempts have been made to link seasonal and annual variations in demographic statistics to the incidence of epidemic diseases, such as plague, as well as to food shortage and variations in weather patterns. Indeed, Penrith has served as a model isolated rural community for England (Howson 1961, Appleby 1973, Duncan et al. 1992, Scott and Duncan 1996, Scott et al. 1998). Included in the above studies are several known malarial parishes, such as Cartmel, Crosthwaite,

Kendal and Kirkham, and others that were highly likely to have suffered the disease, such as Stalmine on the Fylde. Ague, however, notwithstanding its widespread occurrence, was not mentioned as a contributory demographic factor, despite its known devastating impact on populations in the fens and marshes of south-east England (Dobson 1998a,b). It is not inconceivable, given the previous description of the health of the Berwickshire population, that ague had serious implications for rural people in the north, living on the edge of food sustainability. While ague is unlikely to have produced the sharp but isolated peaks in mortality associated with plague, its chronic and continuing debilitating effects on the population of the rural poor in affected areas may have been sufficient to impact on food production, leading to shortage. Furthermore, the effect may have been accentuated by year-to-year variations in temperature or rainfall that reduced crop yields directly or which led to increased mosquito populations, a higher incidence of the disease and a lessened ability to work the land. Challands (1978), in a notable exception to the above demographic studies, highlighted the rapid increase of baptisms and a smaller initial decline in burials in Crosthwaite parish, north of Keswick, from 1770 onwards. She suggested that this might be associated with a decline in the number of deaths caused by ague as a result of the drainage of swampy areas and the increasing availability of medicines.

Some previous views on the causes of ague

From very early days there was widespread recognition that ague was most prevalent in low-lying, poorly-drained areas of countryside such as marshes, swamps, shallow bodies of open water and sluggish-flowing water. Such areas were often damp and frequently subject to mists arising over the open water. Marsh gases, such as hydrogen sulphide and methane, emanating from the marsh, gave a characteristic putrid smell and produced natural phenomena like will o' the wisp. Ague was thought to be carried on these vapours or 'miasma' arising from these marshes. Indeed the epithet malaria, which was later applied more precisely to the disease, literally meant bad air in its original usage.

Some more local explanations are found within Cumbria. Perhaps the most fanciful reason for the cause of ague, from around Wasdale, was that its appearance coincided with the sporadic sighting, usually during autumn, of a mysterious fish, the botling, in streams entering Wastwater (Palmer 1905). It appears that the mythical botling was large, always male and had a hooked lower jaw. This description suggests strongly that it was the ferox form of brown trout, although exactly how it dispensed ague is left to the imagination.

At a more mundane level there was a widespread belief that the consumption of potatoes, a new crop that was beginning to be more widely planted in Cumbria, was a cause of ague. More enlightened observers suggested that consumption of potatoes indicated a poor diet low in fresh vegetables which made the poor less resistant to seasonal afflictions such as ague (Scott 1899, Bouch and Jones 1961, Scott and Duncan 1996). A ditty about potatoes, published in the *Carlisle Patriot* of 1870, runs

> ... And predicted tales were spread
> That they endangered life
> For where they most were used as food
> The ague was most rife ....
>
> (Anon 1870)

By contrast, Hodgson (1810) in his *Description of Westmorland* noted that in Kendal '... the introduction of tea, potatoes and wheat and new modes of agriculture have prevailed over the old system, and agues have disappeared'. Robertson (1911), in his *Wordsworth and the English Lake Country*, wrote that a poor winter diet of salmon, salt beef and salt mutton was thought to cause ague in the following spring but that the introduction of tea and coffee contributed to its decline.

Even among learned people there was confusion as to where ague originated. At a public meeting in Staveley, to discuss the proposed new Kentmere reservoir in 1845, Mr Read, a surgeon, '... offered the pertinent observations on the value of the proposed reservoirs in removing the malaria of the rivers that existed at certain seasons of the year' (Anon 1845b). This appears to imply that creating a new body of still water might reduce malaria, a suggestion at odds with knowledge today. By contrast, an instruction from the Board of Health on the application of sewage onto agricultural land warned that ' ... the common practice of irrigation with plain water is often productive of ague' particularly near dwellings (Anon 1852a).

Ague in the north-country dialect

Historically, several local dialect words have been used to indicate an infection by the ague, suggesting that the disease was sufficiently common to warrant its own vocabulary. One of the commonest words in Westmorland and Cumberland was *shakin* or *shakkins*, which alluded to the major symptom of the disease (Wheeler 1802, Smith 1839, Prevost 1905). An example of its usage is by Robins (1864) in the dialect story *Black Moss, A Tale by a Tarn* in which a miner asks of someone 'has't got t'shakin ?' In Cumberland the words *ayga* (or *aga*) and *yigga* are recorded from the south-west and north-east of the county respectively (Dickinson 1859, Anderson 1864). *Ayga* becomes *agah* in the Craven district of Yorkshire (Carr 1828). Other North Country words for ague include *aixes* or *axes* and *sheks* or *shekils* (Brockett 1825, Halliwell 1862, Anderson 1864, Wright 1880). In Lancashire and Craven the word *gry* or *graw* was used, respectively, to indicate an ague fit (Bobbin 1828, Carr 1828, Picton 1865).

Local folk remedies and doubtful cures

One source writes that '... agues were so common [amongst the labouring poor of Westmorland] that the frequency of them persuaded vulgar credulity into a belief that the effects of the disorder were beneficial to young persons' (Gough 1827). To the majority, however, ague was an affliction to be cured. There was a widely-held belief that village wise men or women could cure ague (Jackson 1809, Porter 1876, Findler 1968, Rollinson 1974, Sydney 2009). An example comes from the annals of the Henry family of Cheshire in which Mary Savage '... learnt a remedy for agues which her mother said made her recognised as a sort of 'doctoress to many' (Crawford 1984). There was a belief that those shivering and shaking with the ague were possessed of the devil and that casting out of the ague could be achieved by exorcism, a task undertaken by the village wise person (Harland and Wilkinson 1867).

It is not surprising, therefore, that a multiplicity of spells, potions, charms and magic was employed to treat the disease and its symptoms, all needless to say with doubtful effect (Forbes 1971). Fig. 14 (page 45) shows, for example, the title page of Mason's 1745 treatise on the *Nature of an Intermitting Fever and Ague Considered* which, while recognising the effectiveness of bark as a cure (see following section), also listed a number of dubious treatments. These included 'Spirits, Acids, Charms, Frights, Emeticks, Catharticks, Sudorificks, Hot and Cold Bathing'.

Collingwood (1906) discussed a book of spells and magical receipts taken from a moss trooper in Carlisle in 1685 within which a cure for ague is to apply '… a few barbarous characters [runes] to the body of the party distemper'd'. There was a belief that because ague was a disease of damp areas it could be treated with herbs, such as bog-bean (*Menyanthes trifoliata*), collected in the locality from which it was thought to arise (Palmer 1914). Similarly, the leaves of trembling aspen (*Populus tremula*) were carried as a charm against ague. The trembling of the leaves, even at low wind speed, resembled the shaking during an ague fit (Henderson 1879).

A written charm entitled *Remedy for a Feavour or an Ague*, from the commonplace book of Christopher Birkett of Troutbeck (Scott 1904, Rollinson 1974), is typical of similar crucifixion charms that were frequently employed in Cumbria and are to be found elsewhere in England (Brand and Ellis 1813, Davies 1996, Levack 2001). It was intended to be worn on the chest and was reputed to protect the wearer against ague. It stated that

> When Jesus did see the Crosse whereon his body should be crucified, his body did shake. The Jews did aske him if he had an Ague. He answered and said whosoever keepeth this in mind or in writing shall never be troubled with an Ague nor a feavour, soe Lord help thy servants, they that put their trust in thee.

George Sandford, vicar of Church Minshall, collected a similarly-worded charm from an old parishioner in Cheshire, who professed '… to have wrought many cures' (Sandford 1849).

Another magical charm as a cure for ague, also to be worn around the neck, was noted down by both Elizabeth Birkett and Benjamin Browne of Troutbeck in their common place books in the late seventeenth century. This charm involved writing down the word 'Abracadabra' 11 times, successively removing a letter so that the final version consisted of just the letter 'a' (Birkett 1699, Nicolson 2012).

Metal charm bracelets were also worn by the rural working poor in the eighteenth century to ward off the ague (fig. 10). A good example of such a copper alloy bracelet was found at Brampton in the Eden Valley, just north of Appleby in an area where ague was known to have occurred.[34] This bracelet is of an unsophisticated

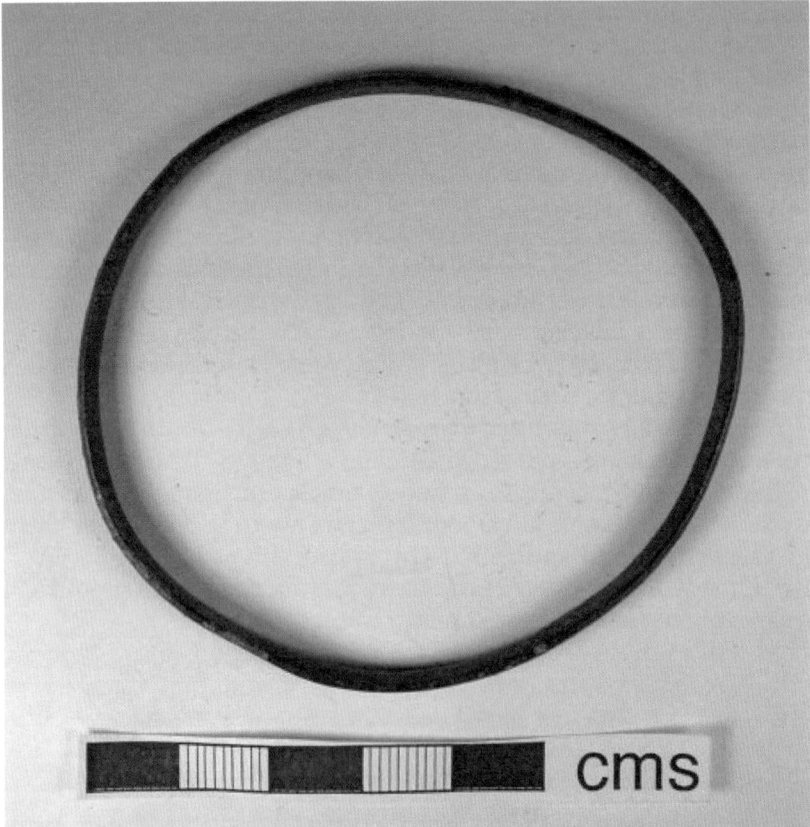

Fig. 10. Eighteenth-century ague bracelet from Brampton near Appleby (Courtesy of the Portable Antiquities Scheme).

design and is decorated with a simple groove. In some places, such as Lincolnshire, eel-skin bracelets or garters served a similar function, again reinforcing the idea that cures/preventatives for ague were best sought in wetland areas (Anon 1900a).

A contrasting remedy by Elizabeth Birkett, also from Troutbeck, contained within her manuscript 'commonplace and recipe book' of 1699, instructs '... Take a spider and lye it quick on a cloth and hang it quick about the Party's neck, they not knowing of it, and take it away when the fit is over' (Birkett 1699). Such folk remedies for ague involving the application of spiders' webs, carrying spiders in bags, and swallowing spiders with the legs removed are widespread in Lancashire and England generally (Wilkinson 1861, Harland 1858).

Indeed, as late as 1809, a Dr. Robert Jackson of County Durham was still arguing in the medical literature the case for the ingestion of spiders' webs as a cure for recalcitrant cases of ague, based on his observations of its use by a 'wise' woman (Jackson 1809). The regular ingestion of spiders as a cure for ague appears to have been associated with the English physician Thomas Mouffet (1553-1604) to whom Little Miss Muffet of nursery rhyme fame, with her morbid fear of spiders, is attributed. In some parts of the country a caterpillar, rather than a spider, was carried in the pocket on the assumption that as it shrivelled the ague would disappear (Henderson 1879).

Other cures involved making invocations to the Holy Trinity over three horseshoes nailed upright, and tying locks of hair to the branches of black poplar trees, to name but a few (e.g. Anon 1898, Collingwood 1903, Gutch and Peacock 1908). One particularly gruesome cure is described in *The House and Farm accounts of the Shuttleworths of Gawthorpe Hall*, near Padiham, Lancashire (Harland 1858). It notes that 'The chips or cuttings of a gibbet or gallows, on which one or more persons have been executed or exposed, if worn next to the skin or round the neck in a bag, will prevent or cure ague'.

By contrast, gentlefolk of ample means could avail themselves of 'medicinal' spring water. One such spa, the Holy Well spring, on Humphrey Head near Grange-over-Sands, was reputed to cure agues and a range of other diseases (fig.11). Visitors travelled long distances to bathe in and drink its mineral waters. Notable visiting families included the Fells of Swarthmoor Hall in 1674 and the Brownes of Troutbeck in 1779, both of whom we know were touched by the ague (Leigh 1700, Barber 1894, Gambles 1993). Treatment was expensive: Sarah Fell's account book reveals a cost of nine shillings for access to the waters. Similar 'cures' for the ague were claimed for several other northern springs. In what is now Dumfries and Galloway there were reputedly therapeutic springs at Barnbarroch near Kirkinner and at Laurieston, while in Northumberland there were equivalent 'healing' springs at Longwitton and Wark (Wallis 1769, Lewis 1844, Anon 1845a). In Cheshire springs at St. Stephen's Well in Delamere Forest and at Whitlebitch Well near Utkinton were promoted as cures for ague (GW 1600, Ormerod 1819). It is notable that several of these waters were chalybeate springs, rich in iron, possibly an attractive and beneficial feature to those anaemic from the effects of ague. Lack of iron may also explain the reports of ague-affected communities in south Berwickshire occasionally resorting to drinking the blood of their cattle (Grierson 1839).

Fig. 11. St Agnes Well or Holy Well on Humphrey Head showing the associated building (now demolished). The mineral water was formerly used as a treatment for ague. The well is about halfway along the peninsula on the western side (Courtesy of the *Heritage Photo Archive and Heritage Image Register*).

Traditional herbal medicines were frequently used in northern England to treat ague. Many options of doubtful efficacy were available, such as fever-few (*Tanacetum parthenium*), taken as a posset drink while fasting, or cinquefoil (*Potentilla erecta*), gathered at the right phase of the moon and taken as a powder in white wine (Harland 1858). One treatment (fig. 12) from the Fleming family of Rydal Hall instructs '... Take 2 handfulls of Ash Keys, one of Cammomil. Infuse for 48h° in Tab. Beer. Take a good drought about ¼ of an hour before the fit comes, then walk and use moderate exercise'.[11] Another, from the same source, recommends '... Carduus Benedictus Possets which makes them sweat much and which lessens the number of cold

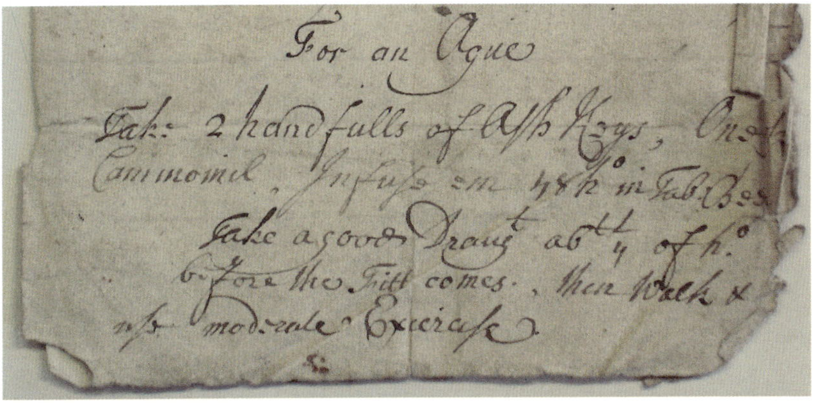

Fig. 12. Treatments for ague. *Above*. Recipe from the Fleming family of Rydal Hall (17th C) (Courtesy of Cumbria Archives, Kendal). *Below*. A cure for the ague. from the Church Book of Keswick Congregational Church (1750-1800) (Courtesy of Cumbria Archives, Carlisle).

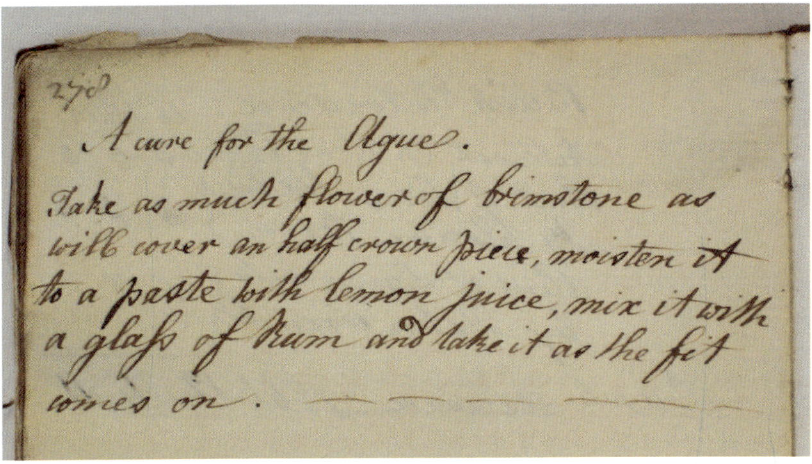

and hot fits'.[12] This involved making an infusion of the herb blessed thistle (*Cnicus benedictus*) in hot sweetened milk curdled with wine or ale.

Citrus fruit also figured prominently among treatments. An early record of its use is in a letter of 1706 to the Rev. Thomas Brockbank of Cartmel who had written earlier to a Mrs Pearson about his wife's ague. She replied that '... I'm sorry that Mrs Brockbank's ague continues. I have sent her a cupple of Cheny Oranges' (Trappes-Lomax 1930). Harland (1858) gives the following recipe from the annals of the Shuttleworth family of Gawthorpe Hall '... Two ounces of the [lemon] juice mixed with the like quantity of spirit of wine, and drunk at the first approach of an ague fit, taketh away the shaking presently, and seldom faileth at the second time of taking perfectly to cure the same'. Even in supposedly more enlightened times ineffectual folk remedies persisted in Cumberland. An article in the *Carlisle Patriot* newspaper in 1829 noted that '... A Seville orange cut into pieces and eaten, peel and all, without more rest than necessary to take breath, is said to be an infallible remedy for ague' (Anon 1829). A cure for the ague in the *Cumberland Packet* in 1786 instructs '... Take as much flower of brimstone [sulphur] as will cover half a crown, moisten it with lemon-juice, mix it with a glass of rum, and take it when the fit come on'. A similar treatment described in the *Lancaster Gazette* of 1824 substitutes a gill of port wine for the rum (Anon 1786, 1824). The Hawkshead parish register for 1784 shows that a sum of 1s. 6p. was provided to purchase '... one gill of Brandy and one quart of ale for Sarah Usher to stop the ague' (Allen 1878). It is likely that the alcohol in many of these treatments was the beneficial element, acting as a palliative rather than an effective cure.

An interesting relic of past treatment for ague was noted in Carlisle. The rare herb costmary (*Tanacetum balsamita*) was found growing in a surviving remnant of the herb garden at the medieval Hospital of St. Nicholas. Costmary was a well-known herbal 'treatment' for ague (Blezard 1962).

A highly novel but ineffectual treatment for ague is given by the Lake Poet Robert Southey in his commonplace book (Warter 1850). He noted that 'Agues, it is said, have not unfrequently been cured by electricity – the mode by drawing sparks through flannel or the clothes for ten minutes, either at the time of the fit or before it is expected'. Electricity at that time was only just coming into common usage.

Another widely used palliative against the ague in the fenlands of eastern England was opium, and poppies were grown extensively for this purpose (Jones 1700, Maynard 1894, Berridge 1977, 1978, Nicholls 2000). It was often consumed as poppy-head tea. While there is little evidence for widespread poppy cultivation in Cumbria (see Newman and Wilson 1951), it is interesting that Southey's fellow Lake Poet Thomas de Quincey, famous for his *Confessions of an Opium Eater*, suffered severe bouts of the ague during early childhood and these persisted for around two years (de Quincey 1854, Page 1877). This period of incapacitating illness had a profound influence on his later life and he may have developed his opium habit as a child while being treated for malaria.

A Lancashire farmer, for devilment, reputedly bequeathed his ague infection to the local parson in his will (Anon 1823). The ague supposedly left the farmer and transferred to the parson, showing either that highly improbable coincidences really do occur or that urban myths were around even in the nineteenth century.

Effective treatments for ague

The most medically effective treatment for ague during the seventeenth to the nineteenth centuries was the natural product quinine, an alkaloid derived from the bark of South American trees of the genus *Cinchona,* variously known in its natural form as Peruvian bark, Jesuits' bark or in pulverised form as Jesuits' or Devil's powder. In the late 1500s Jesuit priests in Peru discovered the fever-reducing properties of the bark of a tree known locally as quina-quina (Keeble 1997). Around the 1630s the bark of another tree, later given the generic name *Cinchona* by Linnaeus in 1742, proved much more effective against various forms of malaria. It was, however, not until the 1820s that the active ingredient in the bark of this tree was identified by two French chemists. Confusingly, they named their compound quinine, after the quina-quina tree rather than after the *Cinchona* from which it was extracted (Meshnick and Dobson 2001, Keeble 1997)(fig.13). Various types of Peruvian *Cinchona* bark were thus imported into Europe for the treatment of ague long before its active ingredient was known. The first officially recorded use in Britain was by Richard Morton (1692) in his *Pyretologia*.

Interestingly, a list of books in Sir James Lowther's library at Flatt Hall (Whitehaven Castle) in 1757 lists as number 733 Sir Richard Talbor's *The English Remedy, or Talbor's Wonderfull Secret in Curing Agues and Fevers* (Talbor 1682, Brownrigg 1993). Talbor's 'miracle cure', which pre-dates Morton, was in fact Peruvian bark but he kept its identity secret to enhance his own reputation as a physician who could cure ague (Keeble 1997). Following a similar theme, a Dr. Lancaster of Sedbergh is listed among the subscribers to the cost of publication of Mason's (1745) treatise on *The Nature of an Intermitting Fever and Ague* (fig.14), a book that details how to treat the condition. It seems highly likely that he had encountered ague within his area of practice. Another interesting Westmorland connection in the story of quinine involves the Crewdson family of Kendal. Maria Crewdson (b.1807),

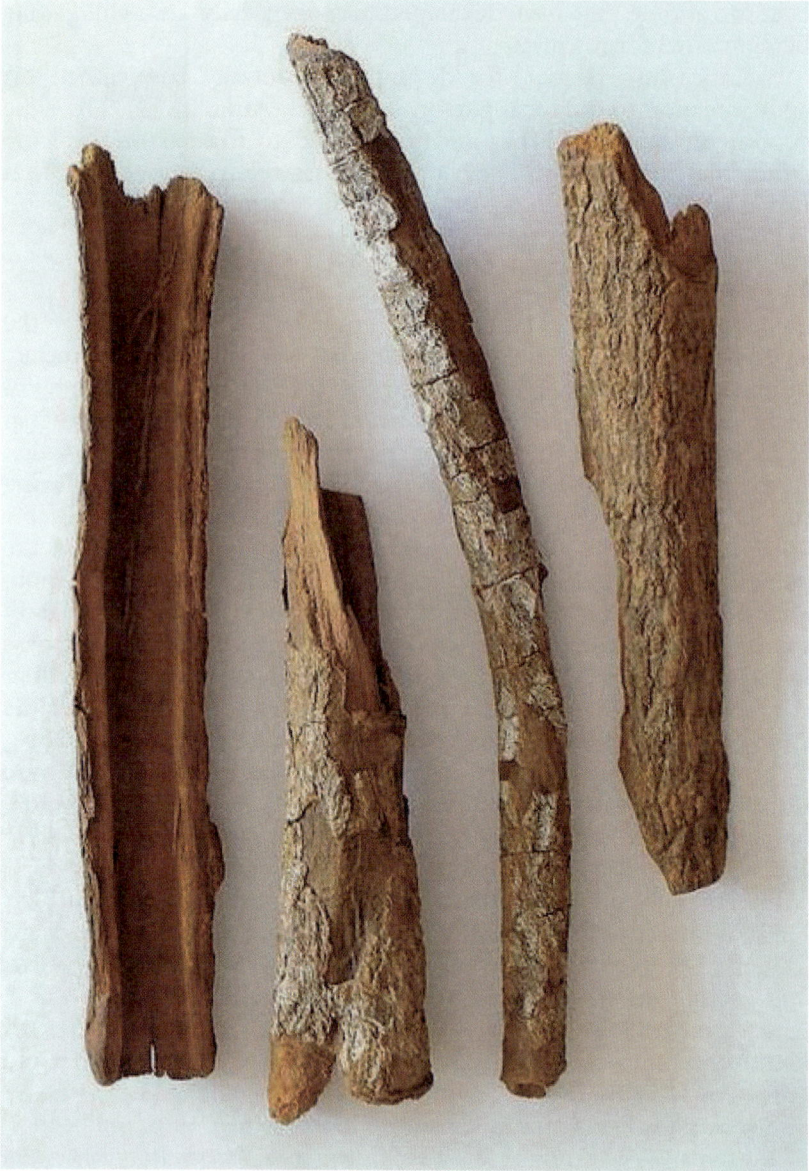

Fig. 13. Peruvian (*Cinchona*) bark (Courtesy of Wikimedia Commons).

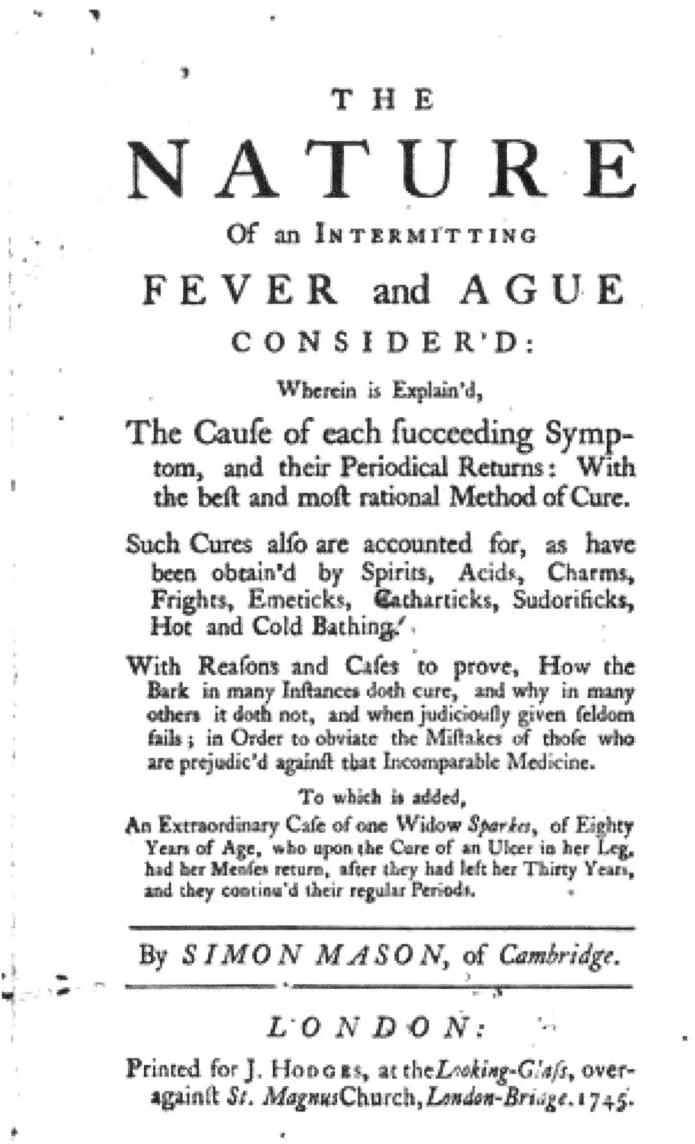

THE

NATURE

Of an INTERMITTING

FEVER and AGUE

CONSIDER'D:

Wherein is Explain'd,

The Caufe of each fucceeding Symptom, and their Periodical Returns: With
the beft and moft rational Method of Cure.

Such Cures alfo are accounted for, as have
been obtain'd by Spirits, Acids, Charms,
Frights, Emeticks, Catharticks, Sudorificks,
Hot and Cold Bathing.

With Reafons and Cafes to prove, How the
Bark in many Inftances doth cure, and why in many
others it doth not, and when judicioufly given feldom
fails; in Order to obviate the Miftakes of thofe who
are prejudic'd againft that Incomparable Medicine.

To which is added,

An Extraordinary Cafe of one Widow *Sparkes*, of Eighty
Years of Age, who upon the Cure of an Ulcer in her Leg,
had her Menfes return, after they had left her Thirty Years,
and they continu'd their regular Periods.

By *SIMON MASON*, of *Cambridge*.

LONDON:

Printed for J. Hodges, at the *Looking-Glafs*, over-
againft *St. Magnus*Church, *London-Bridge*. 1745.

Fig. 14. Title page of Mason's (1745) *Treatise on the Nature of an Intermitting Fever and Ague*, a book to which a Dr. Lancaster of Sedbergh was a listed subscriber.

aunt of William Dilworth Crewdson High Sheriff of Westmorland in1888, whose portrait adorns Kendal Town Hall, married John Elliot Howard, who was to devote his life to the study of the extraction and use of quinine.[33] Fig. 15 shows an old nineteenth century quinine storage bottle from Downward's chemist shop in Ulverston.

Several treatises were subsequently published on the uses and efficacy of different forms of powdered bark (e.g. Saunders 1782, Rigby 1783, Relph 1794, MacCulloch 1828, Fordyce 1895). Around this time patent medicines for the cure of ague became widely available. It is notable that newly-published books on ague and its treatment were advertised in the Cumbrian press (Anon 1787). The recipes for many of these patent medicines was often a closely guarded secret and it is uncertain that they all contained bark or quinine in therapeutic doses, although some state this explicitly in the name. Several brands were in direct competition, often making exaggerated claims or with published testimonials as to their efficacy. Perusal of the advertisement section of the Cumbrian newspapers of the time shows that patent cures for ague were regularly advertised across the breadth of the county (fig. 16). A few of the many examples to be found, often repeated in several different newspaper titles, including the *Westmorland Gazette* and *Kendal Mercury*, are summarised in Table 1, spanning the period from 1777-1877. Prices were not cheap, with the smallest bottles/pill boxes selling for over one shilling, putting them beyond the reach of the poorest families. The

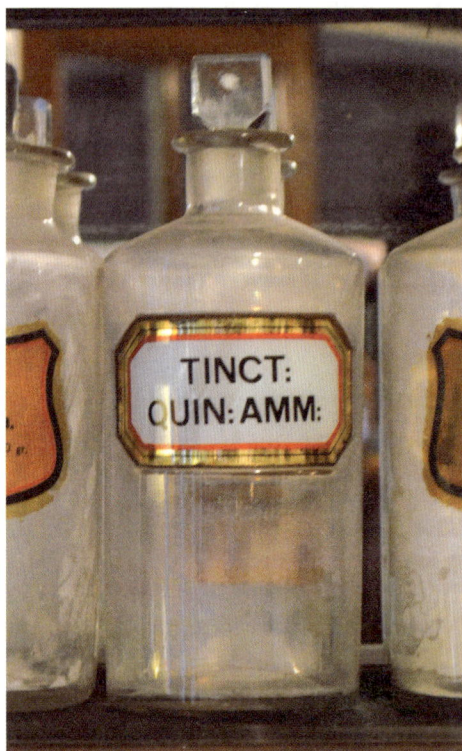

Fig. 15. Nineteenth-century quinine bottle from John Downwards' chemist shop in Ulverston (Courtesy of the Museum of Lakeland Life, Kendal).

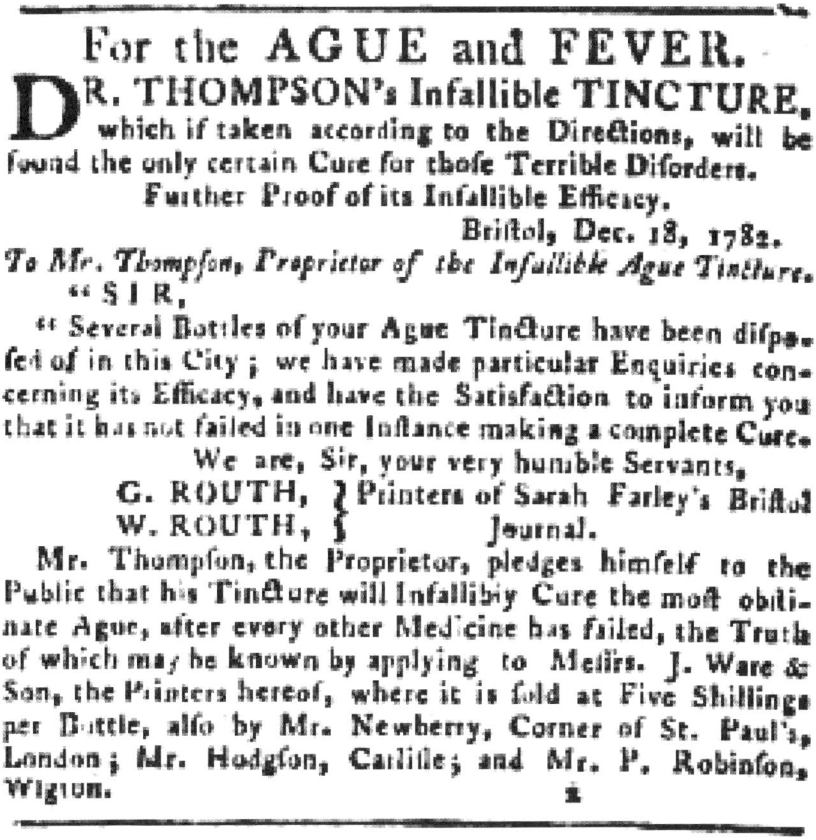

For the **AGUE** and **FEVER.**

DR. THOMPSON's Infallible **TINCTURE,**
which if taken according to the Directions, will be
found the only certain Cure for thofe Terrible Diforders.
Further Proof of its Infallible Efficacy.

Briftol, Dec. 18, 1782.

To Mr. Thompfon, Proprietor of the Infallible Ague Tincture.
"SIR,
" Several Bottles of your Ague Tincture have been difpo-
fed of in this City ; we have made particular Enquiries con-
cerning its Efficacy, and have the Satisfaction to inform you
that it has not failed in one Inftance making a complete Cure.
We are, Sir, your very humble Servants,
G. ROUTH, } Printers of Sarah Farley's Briftol
W. ROUTH, } Journal.
Mr. Thompfon, the Proprietor, pledges himfelf to the
Public that his Tincture will Infallibiy Cure the moft obfti-
nate Ague, after every other Medicine has failed, the Truth
of which may he known by applying to Meffrs. J. Ware &
Son, the Printers hereof, where it is fold at Five Shillings
per Bottle, alfo by Mr. Newberry, Corner of St. Paul's,
London ; Mr. Hodgfon, Carlifle; and Mr. P. Robinfon,
Wigton.   2

Fig. 16. Patent medicines: An early advertisement for 'Thompson's Infallible
Tincture for the Ague' appearing in the *Cumberland Paquet and Ware's Whitehaven
Advertiser* in 1783.

question of quackery frequently raised its head and newspapers such
as the *Westmorland Gazette* sometimes carried strong repudiations,
such as a defence of Professor Holloway's Pills as a cure for ague
(Anon 1859). This same newspaper, however, also published a
serious article about the overexploitation of Peruvian bark and the
drastic consequences of a failure of supply (Anon 1862b).

Sometimes it is difficult to ascertain whether effective or quack
medicines were being proffered. For example, Daffy's Elixir (fig.
17), lacked any effective ingredient against ague and it was probably
just the high-spirit alcohol content that made the patient feel better
(Homan 2006). Curwen (1900) wrote that in Kendal '... about

Table 1. Examples of patent medicines to treat ague advertised in Cumbria's newspapers.

Patent Medicine	Date	Price of smallest bottle/box	Newspaper where advertised
Turlington's Balsam of Life	1750	3s 6d	Pamphlet (Anon 1750)
Dr Bateman's Original Pectoral Drops	1777		*Cumberland Paquet and Ware's Whitehaven Advertiser (CPWWA)*
Dr Thompson's Infallible Tincture	1783 1788	2s 6d	*CPWWA*
Dalby's Ague Tincture	1790	1s 1½d	*CPWWA*
Daffy's Elixir	1792	1s 6d	*CPWWA*
Rookes Matchless Balsam	1794		*CPWWA*
Tower's Fluid Extract of Bark	1831	2s 9d	*CPWWA*
Moxon and Smith's New Tonic Tincture	1832 1837	2s 9d	*Carlisle Patriot Carlisle Journal*
Harvey's Bark Pills with Sasparilla	1839		*CPWWA*
Holloway's Pills	1843	1s 1½d	*CPWWA*
Holloway's Pills	1846		*Carlisle Patriot*
Wordsell's Vegetable Pills	1857	1s 1½d	*Whitehaven News*
Quinine Wine	1870	2s 3d	*Cumberland and Westmorland Advertiser and Penrith Chronicle*
Pepper's Quinine and Iron Tonic	1877		*CPWWA*

Fig. 17. Patent medicines: an early Daffy's tincture bottle (Courtesy of the Royal Pharmaceutical Society Museum).

1790 a certain Doctress Wood came down from London to settle amongst us a most marvellous practitioner in physic and midwifery'. A handbill announcing her arrival in Kendal (fig. 18) claimed that 'She cures the ague, though of a long continuance, in a short time'.

Other natural plant products had been tested by physicians for their fever-reducing properties in cases of ague and some success in treatment was claimed. Examples promoted in the Cumbrian press included the flowers of red star-thistle (*Centaurea calcitrapa*), the flowers and seeds of lesser nettle (*Urtica urens*) and southern blue-gum (*Eugalyptus globulus*), but their efficacy remains essentially unproven (Anon 1797, 1819, 1872). William Brownrigg, the Whitehaven physician, mentioned the efficacy of conessi bark, from the tropical Asian tree *Holarrhena pubescens*, as an effective cure for ague in the mid-1700s, although it was more typically used against dysentery (Brownrigg 1993).

By HIs MAJESTY's Royal AUTHORITY.

TO THIS PLACE IS COME

Doctress WOOD,

(From LONDON)

Practitioner in Phyfic and Midwifery,

WHO, by many years experience, has attained the art and knowledge of curing moft curable diftempers incident to the human body. She gives patients her advice at firft fight, by informing them whether their diforders are curable or not, and will not take them in hand if incurable, on any confideration whatever, it being known to every one who is acquainted with her, that her fole aim is to do good to her fellow creatures, particularly in that charitable work of giving fight to thofe who are almoft blind, in which her practice has, by GOD's blefling, been attended with very great fuccefs. She cures wounds in any part of the body, ulcers, cancers, king's-evil, or old running fores. She has a fpeedy and never-failing cure for the bloody flux, and convulfion fits. She cures the gravel and ftone, and all manner of deafnefs, provided the drum of the ear is not broken;. great numbers of people who have been deaf many years have been brought to their perfect hearing by her. She cures the ague, though of a long continuance, in a fhort time. She cures the fcurvy, rheumatifm, yellow jaundice, hyfteric fits, or fits of the mother and fpleen, and can cure the nerves ; and thofe who have loft the ufe of their limbs, by colds or otherwife, fhe reftores to their former ufe in a fhort time. She cures coughs, confumptions, inward decays, rickets in children, ruptures, or broken bellies in young or old. 'She cures fiftulas and piles, alfo hard or foft corns in any part of the feet or toes. She cures hair-lips, fcald heads, and wens. She has alfo a fpeedy and never-failing cure for the venereal difeafe, and cures it though of ever fo long a continuance, in a very fhort time. ' She has alfo a famous medicine for the tooth-ach, which cures all diforders in the mouth and gums, and in a few times ufing will be fenfibly perceived ; and with a little continuance will perfectly cure the fcurvy in the gums, and take off all difagreeable fmell from the breath. She alfo prepares the true Scots pills, and difpofes of them, wholefale or retail, at a reafonable price. She has alfo a famous medicine for deftroying worms in young or old, and cures other many grievous diforders, too tedious here to enumerate ; having had great practice, attended with great fuccefs in many defperate cafes ; taking none in hand but whom fhe can perfectly cure.—Pray apply foon, that I may have time to prepare for the operation, and fee the cure performed.

N. B. You may have any of the above medicines when the bill is called for.— Pray keep it clean.—Advice given to the poor GRATIS, by'

DOCTRESS WOOD,

Fig. 18. Handbill advertising the arrival of Doctress Wood in Kendal around 1790. (Reproduced from Curwen's *Kirkbie Kendal*, 1900).

Reasons for the decline of ague

No single factor appears responsible for the decline of ague as a widespread disease in Britain. People were aware of its association with marshy areas but were largely ignorant of the fact that it was a blood disease transmitted by mosquitos. A coming together of circumstances gradually reduced the ability of malaria to survive and prosper in its former habitats. Initially a major factor was wide-scale drainage, carried out to improve land for agriculture, rather than to drain pestilent marshes *per se* (Forbes 1836, Chadwick 1842, Anon 1843b, James 1929, Williamson 2006). A beneficial effect, nevertheless, was the reduction of aquatic habitats available for mosquito breeding, especially in rural areas (Dobson 1998b).

The Inclosure Acts and Awards, relating to the ownership of common land, often ensured that the new owners were able to provide the necessary investment in drainage and improvement to reduce the areas suitable for mosquito breeding. This link between drainage and the decline of ague appears as a recurrent theme throughout Cumbria and the UK generally. Thus, at a meeting of the Windermere Agricultural Society in 1853, the chairman felt able to fete the lord lieutenant of the county, who was in attendance, for his enthusiastic efforts at drainage – emphasising the huge benefits of such drainage for the improved health of the population (Anon 1953c). At Kelso, an ague hotspot in Scotland, Craig (1876) noted that '... cases of the ague, which had formerly been of frequent occurrence, had entirely ceased after these and later draining operations at Berrymoss (now the racecourse) had removed the last of the stagnant morasses of the district'. These benefits were elegantly summarised, with great ecological perception, for the Carse of Gowrie in Perthshire by Dr James Robertson who concluded that following improvement '... the rushes, the lapwing, and ague have now totally disappeared' (Robertson 1799, Philip 1895). Kuhn *et al.* (2003) more recently provide some statistical support for a relationship, in both space and time, between the declining area of wetland and the reduced incidence of malaria in Britain.

Despite the known beneficial effects of drainage, there was some apparent reluctance among Cumbrian farmers to drain land. Walter White (1859) in his *Northumberland and the Border*, expressed some surprise at seeing newly-drained land on Hartside above Langwathby. He intimated that '... your Cumbrian farmer of the old school ... would as soon have a tooth drawn as drain his wet land ... it was better to suffer from damp and ague than to commit the wickedness of draining'.

Coupled with the drainage there were other important changes in agricultural practice (James 1929). In particular, there was a trend away from overwintering cattle in barns in close proximity to human habitation. Such barns, which were often poorly ventilated, provided ideal overwintering and feeding stations for mosquitoes. Lime-washing the inside walls of buildings also began to make them less attractive as resting places for mosquitoes. It has been suggested that increased stocking densities of healthier cattle, resulting from higher agricultural productivity on improved land away from human habitation, provided a more attractive and reliable source of a blood meal, thereby reducing mosquito feeding on humans (Dobson 1998b). Again there is some statistical support for this suggestion (Kuhn et al. 2003).

Within towns and villages, with their greater concentration of potential human hosts for malaria, there was an increasing awareness that insanitary conditions, including open pools, cesspits, open sewers and slowly-flowing drains, not to mention stagnant streams and adjacent rivers, were the breeding grounds for many diseases including ague (Anon 1839,1842, 1845c, Chadwick 1842). A report into sanitary conditions in Aberdeen, for example, recommended '... the drainage of any open common or waste land which appeared ... injuriously to affect the health of the inhabitants, or to cause ague' (Kilgour and Galen 1842). Consequently, in the early- to mid-nineteenth century there was a general movement towards cleaning up the town environment and again this contributed to the decline in ague by the removal of mosquito-breeding sites. Newspapers of the time carried reports on the poor sanitary conditions in several Cumbrian towns including Whitehaven, Carlisle, Keswick and Ulverston and made recommendations for improvement (Anon 1845c, 1852c, 1863b). The *Carlisle Patriot* of 1829, for example, even reproduced a prescriptive list of hygiene advice, first published in *The Lancet*, for the prevention of fever (Anon 1829). Such advice, however, was frequently ignored. Even as late as 1927, fear of ague, transmitted by nuisance populations of *A. claviger* mosquitoes at Cathcart, Renfrewshire, resulted in a court order that a landowner must clear and maintain his ditches (Anon 1927).

Better hygiene, supported by enhanced levels of nutrition, nevertheless, began to improve the general health of the population thereby increasing their ability to resist the debilitating effects of ague (Dobson 1998b). Another suggested factor in the decline of the disease was the increasing recognition of quinine as an effective treatment, and its wider availability through public dispensaries that ministered to the poorer members of society (Durham 1901, Loudon 1981, James 1929, Dobson 1989). However, Dobson later questioned whether quinine was sufficiently widely available to impact on the epidemiology of the disease (Dobson 1998b). This view is given some support by information on the workings of medical practices in Lancashire between 1750 and 1840 (King 2001). The doctors of the time were often sufficiently confident in their use of Jesuits' powder to feel it unnecessary to write down its dosage formulation but also did not keep precise records of the conditions they were treating (King 2001). Dr. Loxham of the Fylde charged patients according to their perceived ability to pay. His fee for treating non-infectious 'fevers', however, ranged from 3s. 6p. to 10s. 6p. and it is unsurprising that his patients were drawn predominantly from the professional and trade classes, who comprised just a small minority of the population (King 2001).

Ague and climate: past and future

There is some evidence that the spread of malaria throughout Europe during the Holocene was linked to changing environmental parameters, particularly the increasing availability of suitable mosquito habitats, coupled with increased movements of people (Sallares 2006). Consequently, there is currently much interest in the possible re-emergence of vivax malaria in the British Isles as a result of climate change (Ramsdale and Gunn 2005). Some mathematical modelling of the potential spread of malaria has been conducted but this is largely based on the effects of climate on the development rate, distribution and abundance of one vector mosquito species *A. atroparvus* (Gill, 1921, Lindsay and Joyce 2000, Lindsay et al. 2010). These models suggest that ague may potentially return to its former haunts in the fenlands and the Kent marshes but is unlikely to reach far into northern England or Scotland (see also Chin and Welsby 2015). Lindsay and Joyce further argued that a series of cold summers in the 1800s may have contributed to the disappearance of ague in the first place. The results, however, appear simplistic and do not sit easily alongside historical information on the former distribution of indigenous ague, which, as shown here, occurred much more widely throughout the northern British Isles.

Little attention is given in the literature to the potential for wind-dispersal by vector species of *Anopheles* and it is assumed that infected females only move at most a distance of a few kilometres. They may, however, move much greater distances. It appears likely, for example, that wind-blown individuals of *A. atroparvus*, originating in France, were responsible for the original introduction of myxomatosis of rabbits into Great Britain at Edenbridge, Kent, in 1953, a leap of around 150km from known sources of infection (Muirhead-Thomson 1956, Sellers 1987, Brugman et al. 2015). Furthermore, the possibility of other, more cool-adapted, *Anopheles* species acting as effective vectors in the north of England and Scotland seems to have been discounted (Blacklock and Carter 1920, see also James 1929).

Ague does not appear to have been as temperature-restricted as these models imply and important attempts to take a wider perspective, such as the work of Duncan (1993) and Reiter (2000) have been largely ignored. Reiter pointed out that the period of decline in malaria in nineteenth-century Britain corresponded with a warming phase that had begun perhaps 100 years earlier and that outbreaks of malaria occurred in Britain during the coldest part of the Little Ice Age, from 1564-1730 AD when malaria was widespread in northern Europe. It is notable that the initial experimental treatment of ague with Peruvian bark in England took place during this colder period. Falling temperatures are thus highly unlikely to explain the decline in ague in Britain: its disappearance, as we have seen, was far more subtle, with the restriction of mosquito habitat through land drainage appearing to be the prime recurrent factor which acted to reduce the ratio of mosquitos to humans to a level insufficient to sustain the disease.

History suggests, as emphasised above, that ague was a much more cosmopolitan disease in Britain than current temperature-based distribution models recognise. Short-term inter-annual variability in climate, nevertheless, appears to have been an important determinant of the seasonal incidence and virulence of ague. Several studies note the relationship between summers with above-average mean temperatures and subsequent increases in the severity of outbreaks of ague (e.g. Creighton 1894, Gill 1921, Dobson 1989). The mechanism is simple: higher temperatures allow mosquitoes to reproduce and develop more quickly, feed more often, and allow a more rapid development of the malarial parasite within the mosquito. This relationship holds as long as suitable wet habitats remain available. Hot summers, however, eventually dry out mosquito habitat. Duncan (1993) argued that in Scotland a combination of wet summers, coupled with above-average temperatures, provided the most potent conditions for malarial outbreaks. She maintained that during the Medieval Warm Period, despite warm temperatures, ague was supressed because of reduced precipitation.

It is fascinating to conclude by asking what lessons might be learned from the historical data on ague and what the future might hold. In Cumbria and elsewhere there are several changes taking place that might potentially affect the possibility of ague returning sometime in the future (Medlock and Vaux 2011). First, there is a pressure to re-wet large areas of former marshlands and poorly-drained habitats. This may involve blocking drains to raise water levels, thereby increasing the value of an area for wetland conservation or river-flow management. Alternatively, it may simply involve switching off drainage pumps as an economy measure forcing a return to the old system of wetland farming, presumably involving lower stock densities. Changes in coastal management practices, such as selective abandonment of sea defences, may produce larger areas of saline marshland suitable for mosquito breeding. Even modifications to the management of existing wetlands, such as removing shade, can lead to a shift in the species composition of the breeding mosquito population (Medlock and Vaux 2011). The second major factor is climate change, with an accelerating trend towards increased mean temperatures for mosquito development and shifts in precipitation patterns, with consequent implications for successful breeding by mosquitoes and the disease they carry. Third, there is an increasing tendency, in some former ague areas, to rear beef cattle intensively in sheds adjacent to human habitation. Collectively, these trends go some way towards re-creating and re-establishing the ideal breeding conditions for mosquitoes that pertained at a time when ague stalked the land! Perhaps more thought and evaluation are required before these trends become fully established. This is particularly pertinent in that on a global scale anopheline mosquitoes are displaying increased resistance to a range of insecticides, malaria in its various forms is becoming increasingly resistant to prophylactic treatments, and the development of highly effective vaccines against malaria is proving elusive.

References

Primary source documents follow a numbering system and are listed under the record office or institution in which they may be found. Published sources follow the Harvard system of referencing.

Primary source documents

Cumbria Archives, Carlisle

1   DFCCL 15/6. Keswick Lake Road Congregational Church. Church book first used by the 'Dissenting Presbyterian Meeting at Keswick'. A cure for the ague. 1750-1800.

2   D HUD 15/12/8. Huddleston Family of Hutton. From Miss Anne Lacey. 1830.

3   Q/11/1/156/2. Cumberland Quarter Sessions. Petition of Eleanora Hewett, widow of John Hewett junior of Sebergham: poor relief. 1728.

4   Q/11/1/158/31. Cumberland Quarter Sessions. Petition of Isabel Hudless, widow of Thomas Hudless, late miller of Cumcatch Mill p. Brampton: poor relief till 'God be pleas'd to Restore her to health again ... to work for her poor Children.' 1730.

5   Q/11/1/165/28. Cumberland Quarter Sessions. Petition of Margaret Reay of 'Irdington' [Irthington], widow: rise in relief. 1732.

6   Q/11/1/171/9. Cumberland Quarter Sessions. Petition of Edward Hetherington of 'Massalen' p. Farlam: poor relief. 1733-34.

7   Q/11/1/181/13. Cumberland Quarter Sessions. Petition of Mabel, widow of the late Richard Gardiner of Brampton parish: poor relief for her partial support. 1736.

8   Q/11/1/188/25. Cumberland Quarter Sessions. Petition of Jane, widow of Christopher Addison of Kirklinton Middle Quarter: poor relief for self and her two children. 1738.

9   Q/11/1/189/1. Cumberland Quarter Sessions. Petition of Jane Addison, widow, of Kirklinton Middle Quarter. 1738.

10 Q/11/1/267/22. Cumberland Quarter Sessions. Copy of inquest into the death of William Barnes in the county gaol in Carlisle who died of the 'ague' having suffered 8 or 9 weeks. 1863.

Cumbria Archives, Kendal

11 WDRY/4/9/18. Le Fleming Family of Rydal Hall. For an Ague. Undated 17th C.

12 WDRY/5/4289. Le Fleming Family of Rydal Hall. Sir D.F. to Sir Cristopher Musgrave. March 28, 1692.

13 WQ/SR/10/4. Westmorland Quarter Sessions. Appleby: Christmas: Petitions roll (part 1): William Abram [of Drybeck]. 1729-1730.

14 WQ/SR/266/28-29. Westmorland Quarter Sessions. Appleby: Christmas: sessions roll: Alexander Cowen. 21 October 1756.

15 WQ/SR/326/30-31. Westmorland Quarter Sessions. Appleby: Michaelmas: sessions roll: John Cairns. 2 October 1766.

Cumbria Archives, Whitehaven

16 YTHOS 2/2/1 and 2/2/2. Annual Reports of the Whitehaven Dispensary 1783-1822.

Derbyshire Record Office, Matlock

17 D1322/Z1. Copy recipes from Wright of Eyam. For an ague. 18-19th Century.

18 D2380A/P1/1/4c. General registers of Parish of Baslow St. Anne. Remedies for the ague and gout. Undated 1752-1804.

19 D2732/1. Manor of Snelston, court book p.12. Letter requesting relief for deserted wife of William Barnes, ill of a third day ague. 1680.

20 5336/2/26/7. Pares of Leicester and Hopwell Hall, Manuscript recipe book. For the ague. 17th Century.

Flintshire Record Office, Hawarden

21 D-G/181/31. Letter from Roger Kenrick to Sir John Trevor concerning widow Roberts and her children, all with tertian ague. 22 Mar 1670/1.

Greater Manchester County Record Office, Bury

22 A9/6. Bury Union Workhouse Admissions Registers. 1864-1907.

Lancashire Archives, Preston

23 ARR/1/2/159. Compert Book: All Deaneries 1765-1766.

24 DDB 61/6 and 61/7. Parker Family of Browsholme. Joseph Pease, Morton upon Swale, to his brother Ambrose Barcroft, Foulrigg. 1668/9 and 1669.

25 DDHK – Hawkshead-Talbot of Chorley. Recipe for a cure for an ague. ca 1728.

26 DDKE/HMC/127. Letter from Alexander Rigby to his brother, George Rigby, at Peel. 16 Sep. 1631.

27 QSB/1/266/52. ASHTON-in-MAKERFIELD – certificate of condition of Alexander Robinson, blind with ague. 1642.

28 QSB/1/266/66. HALSALL – Petition of Cuthbert Frith, linen weaver, burst his bowels and with tertian ague and fever. 1642.

29 QSP/935/4. BARNACRE – Relief for Jane and Elizabeth Wilson with Kentish Ague. c.1705/6.

Northumberland Archives, Woodhorn

30 ZMI/S/77/18/4 and 5. Letters from Ellen Carlyle 1830-1843 in the estate collection of the Middleton family.

West Yorkshire Archive, Wakefield

31 QS1/14/8/6/4. Petition of Anne Askwith of Clint, for relief from herself, husband in an ague and four children. 5 October 1675.

Other sources

32 Abernethy Letter. Letter from Dr Abernethy to Mr Hood regarding the treatment of his ague. Kelso, 19 June 1724. Offered for sale by Richard M. Ford Bookseller in 2016.

33 Howard Papers. Manuscripts – *Cinchona*. JEH. Papers relating to John Elliot Howard. Archives of the Royal Botanic Garden, Kew.

34 Portable Antiquities Scheme, LANCUM-CB8F84. Post medieval ague bracelet.

35 Royal Society Archive. RB/2/30/38. Report by Duke of York concerning ague in Scotland.

Published sources

Allen, J. (1878) 'The earlier registers and parish accounts at Hawkshead', *Transactions of the Cumberland and Westmorland Antiquarian and Archaeological Society, Series 1*, 4, 33-40.

Anderson, R. (1864) *Ballads in the Cumberland Dialect, with Notes, Descriptive of the Manners and Customs of the Cumberland Peasantry: a Glossary of Local Words and a Life of the Author'*, B. Stewart, Carlisle.

Anon (1748) 'Turlington's Balsam', *The Penny Post or the Morning Advertiser*, 20 May, p. 4.

Anon (1750) *Turlington's Balsam of Life*, Turlington's of Lombard Street, London.

Anon (1786) 'A cure for the ague'. *Cumberland Pacquet, and Ware's Whitehaven Advertiser*, 6 December, p. 3.

Anon (1787) 'Advertisement for S. Thomson's book entitled A treatise on the intermittens febris, commonly called the ague and fever', *Cumberland Pacquet, and Ware's Whitehaven Advertiser*, 23 May, p. 1 and 11 July, p. 1.

Anon (1797) 'New febrifuge' *Cumberland Pacquet, and Ware's Whitehaven Advertiser*, 7 February, p. 4.

Anon (1819). 'New febrifuge plant', *Westmorland Advertiser and Kendal Chronicle*, 21 August, p. 3.

Anon (1821) 'Carlisle Dispensary Report', *Carlisle Patriot*, 10 February, p. 3.

Anon (1823) 'Bequeathing the ague', *The Ladies Monthly Museum*, 1 September, p. 146.

Anon (1824) 'The Ague', *Lancaster Gazette*, 16 October 1824, p. 4.

Anon (1826) 'Hints for the holidays', *Blackwood's Edinburgh Magazine*, 20, 1-12.

Anon (1829) 'Cure for the ague', *Carlisle Patriot*, 9 May, p. 3.

Anon (1839) 'Inquiry as to the prevalence of the causes of disease, or the sanitary conditions of the poorer classes, as affected chiefly by the situation and construction of their dwellings', *Kendal Mercury*, 7 December, p. 4.

Anon (1840) 'Penrith District Agricultural Society', *Carlisle Patriot*, 3 October, p. 3.

Anon (1842) 'Report on the sanitary condition of the labouring population of Great Britain', *Westmorland Gazette*, 12 November, p. 2.

Anon (1843a) 'Police, Kendal. Joseph Weber', *Kendal Mercury*, 1 April, p. 3.

Anon (1843b) *Local Reports on the Sanitary Condition of the Labouring Population in England, in Consequence of an Inquiry Directed to be made by the Poor Law Commissioners*, W. Clowes and Sons, London.

Anon (1845a) *The New Statistical Account of Scotland by the Ministers of the Respective Parishes Under the Superintendence of a Committee of the Society for the Benefit of the Sons and Daughters of the Clergy*, W. Blackwood and Sons, Edinburgh.

Anon (1845b) 'The proposed reservoir on the Kent. Public meeting at Staveley', *Westmorland Gazette*, 8 March, p. 3.

Anon (1845c) 'Important public meeting on the sanitary condition of Kendale', *Kendal Mercury*, 22 November, p. 2-3.

Anon (1846) 'Kendal water works bill', *Westmorland Gazette*, 9 May, p. 4.

Anon (1847) 'Public Health', *Carlisle Patriot*, 10 December, p. 2.

Anon (1848) 'The Kendal Agricultural Association', *Kendal Mercury*, 21 October, p. 4.

Anon (1849) 'The Kendal sanitary enquiry', *Kendal Mercury*, 16 June, p. 4.

Anon (1850) 'Manners and customs of Lancaster a century ago from the autobiography of a Lancaster Friend', *Westmorland Gazette*, 9 November, p. 4.

Anon (1852a) 'Application of town sewage to agricultural production', *Kendal Mercury*, 17 January, p. 3.

Anon (1852b) *Keswick and its Neighbourhood. A Handbook or the Use of Visitors.* Garnett, Windermere.

Anon (1852c) 'The sanitary condition of Keswick', *Cumberland Paquet and Ware's Whitehaven Advertiser,* 6 April, p. 3.

Anon (1852d) 'Surgeon's report', *Westmorland Gazette,* 30 October, p. 6.

Anon (1853a) 'Board of Health', *Kendal Mercury,* 4 June, p. 6.

Anon (1853b) 'Miscellaneous information', *The Justice of the Peace and Local Government Review,* 17, 527-528.

Anon (1853c) 'Windermere Agricultural Society', *Kendal Mercury,* 15 October, p. 6.

Anon (1854) 'Local Hygiene', *Carlisle Patriot,* 1 April, p. 5.

Anon (1856) 'In memory of Esthwaite Lake', *Westmorland Gazette,* 6 November, p. 5.

Anon (1859) 'The logic of fact and experience', *Westmorland Gazette,* 2 July, p. 7.

Anon (1860) 'Sanitary reform at Cockermouth', *Carlisle Journal,* 3 February, p. 8.

Anon (1862a) 'Meeting of the Carlisle Distress Fund Committee', *Carlisle Journal,* 7 October, p. 2.

Anon (1862b) 'Peruvian Bark', *Westmorland Gazette,* 22 November, p. 6.

Anon (1862-1869) *Detailed Reports of the Registrar-General of births deaths and marriages in Scotland,* Murray and Gibb, Edinburgh.

Anon (1863a) 'National Association for the Promotion of Social Science', *Caledonian Mercury,* 14 October, p. 6.

Anon (1863b) 'Sanitary condition of Whitehaven', *Carlisle Journal,* 18 August, p. 2.

Anon (1864a) 'Maude's Meadow drain. Cutting the first sod', *Westmorland Gazette,* 20 August, p. 6.

Anon (1864b) 'Sanitary state of Maryport', *Carlisle Journal,* 9 February, p. 2.

Anon (1865) 'Whitehaven Board of Guardians', *Whitehaven News,* 30 November, p. 6.

Anon (1866) 'The sanitary condition of the Union', *Whitehaven News,* 30 August, p. 6.

Anon (1867a) 'Cartmel Church', *Westmorland Gazette,* 21 December, p. 5.

Anon (1867b) 'Died on the road', In both *Westmorland Gazette and Kendal Mercury,* 19 January, pp. 9 and 6 respectively.

Anon (1870) 'Auld Lang Syne in Scotland', *Carlisle Patriot,* 13 May, p. 7.

Anon (1872) '*Eucalyptus globulus* in intermittent fever', *The British Medical Journal* 1, 503-504.

Anon (1882) 'West Somerset Branch: Annual Meeting', *The British Medical Journal,* 2, 230-231.

Anon (1898) 'Spiders a cure for the ague', *Fenland Notes and Queries,* 4, 26.

Anon (1900a) 'Eel-skins in Lincolnshire folk medicine', *The Naturalist, Hull,* 1900, 227.

Anon (1900b) *Report of the Committee Appointed to Inquire Into the Public Health of the City of Dublin.* For Ireland Local Government Board by HMSO, London.

Anon (1904) *Report of the Departmental Committee Appointed by the Local Government Board for Scotland to Inquire into the System of Poor Law Medical Relief and Into the Rules and Regulations for the Management of Poorhouses.* Local Goverment Board for Scotland.

Anon (1927) 'Mosquitoes in Renfrewshire', *The British Medical Journal,* 2, 34.

Anon (1929) 'Bicentenary of the Edinburgh Royal Infirmary', *British Medical Journal,* 2, 321.

Anon (1932) 'Mosquitoes and ague in Scotland, Aberdeenshire 100 years ago'. *Aberdeen Journal,* 7 July, p. 6.

Anon (2015) *Malaria Imported Into the United Kingdom: 2014,* Public Health England, London.

Appleby, A.B. (1973) 'Disease or famine? Mortality in Cumberland and Westmorland 1580-1640', *The Economic History Review*, 26, 403-432.

Ashcroft, L. (2006) *Cleaning up Kendal: a Century of Sanitary History*, Curwen Trust Archive Texts, Kendal.

Ashworth, J.H. (1927) 'The distribution of anopheline mosquitoes in Scotland', *Proceedings of the Royal Society of Edinburgh*, 47, 81-93.

Bagot, A. (1975) 'Monsieur Beaumont and Col. Graham. The making of a garden 1689-1710', *Garden History*, 3, 66-78.

Bailey, J. (1813) *General View of the Agriculture of the County of Durham with Observations on the Means of its Improvement*, Shirley, Neely and Jones, London.

Baines, E. (1834) *A Companion to the Lakes of Cumberland, Westmoreland and Lancashire*, Simpkin and Marshall, London.

Baines, E. (1886) *History of the County Palatine and Duchy of Lancaster, Volume 3*, Fisher, Son and Co., London.

Baines, T. (1867) *Lancashire and Cheshire, Past and Present*, William Mackenzie, London.

Baines, T. (1871) *Yorkshire Past and Present: A History and a Description of the Three Ridings of the Great County of York*, William Mackenzie, London.

Barber, H. (1894) *Furness and Cartmel Notes, or Jottings and Topographical, Ecclesiastical and Popular Antiquities, and of Historical Circumstances, As Well As Interesting Facts Relating to the Districts of Furness and Cartmel*, James Atkinson, Ulverston.

Barbieri, M. (1857) *A Descriptive and Historical Gazetteer of the Counties of Fife, Kinross and Clackmannan*, MacLachlan and Stewart, Edinburgh.

Bayers, W. (1824) 'Medico-topographical sketches of Appleby, Westmoreland, and the adjoining country', *Edinburgh Medical and Surgical Journal*, 22, 320-331.

Begbie, H. (1926) *Life of William Booth: The Founder of the Salvation Army. Volume 1*, Macmillan and Co., London.

Berridge, V. (1977) 'Fenland opium eating in the nineteenth century', *British Journal of Addiction*, 72, 275-284.

Berridge, V. (1978) 'Victorian opium eating: responses to opiate use in nineteenth-century England', *Victorian Studies*, 21, 437-461.

Birkett, E. (1699) *Common Place Book*, Transcription available as a PDF at http://www.nationaltrust.org.uk/townend/features/a-taste-of-townend

Blacklock, R. and Carter, H.F. (1920) 'The experimental infection in England of *Anopheles plumbeus* Stephens and *Anopheles bifurcatus* L., with *Plasmodium vivax*', *Annals of Tropical Medicine and Parasitology*, 13, 413-420.

Blezard, E. (1962) 'The herbs of St. Nicholas', *Cumbria Magazine*, 12, 242.

Bobbin, T. (1828) *Lancashire Dialect and Poems*, Hurst, Chance and Co., London.

Boott, F. (1834) *Memoir of the Life and Medical Opinions of John Armstrong, M.D. to Which is Added an Inquiry into Some of the Facts Connected with Those Forms of Fever Attributed to Malaria or Marsh Effluvium, Volume 2*, Edward Rainford, London.

Bouch, C.M.L. and Jones, G.P. (1961) *A Short Economic and Social History of the Lake Counties, 1500-1830*, Manchester University Press, Manchester.

Boudin, M., Green, H. and Helfft, Dr. (1849) 'On the antagonism of miasmatic fever and pulmonary consumption, and the alleged incompatibility of ague and its causes with pulmonary consumption', *The Edinburgh Medical and Surgical Journal*, 71, 344-380.

Brand, J. and Ellis, H. (1813) *Observations on Popular Antiquities Chiefly Illustrating the Origin of our Vulgar Customs, Ceremonies and Superstitions*, Cadell and Davies, London.

Brockbank, W. and Kenworthy, F. (Eds). (1968) *The Diary of Richard Kay, 1716-51: of Baldingstone, Near Bury, a Lancashire Doctor: Extracts*', Chetham Society, Manchester.

Brockett, J.T. (1825) *A Glossary of North Country Words in Use*. E. Charnley, Newcastle upon Tyne.

Bromley, J. (1879-80) 'The rural life of a Lancashire minister 150 years ago', *Transactions of the Historic Society of Lancashire and Cheshire*, 32, 117-142.

Bromley, J. (1885) 'Extracts from the common place-books of the Rev. Peter Walker', *Transactions of the Historic Society of Lancashire and Cheshire*, 37, 117-140.

Brownrigg, W. (1993) *The Medical Casebook of William Brownrigg, M.D, F.R.S. (1712-1800) of the Town of Whitehaven in Cumberland*, Wellcome Institute for the History of Medicine, London.

Brugman, V.A., Hernandez-Triana, L.M., Prosser, S.W.J., Weland, C., Westcott, D.G., Fooks, A.R. and Johnson, N. (2015) Molecular species identification, host preference and detection of myxoma virus in the *Anopheles maculipennis* complex (Diptera: Culicidae) in southern England, UK. *Parasites and Vectors*, 8:421. DOI 10.1186/s13071-015-1034-8.

Carlisle, N. (1813) *A Topographical Dictionary of Scotland and the Islands in the British Sea*, G. and W. Nicol, London.

Carr, W. (1828) *The Dialect of Craven in the West Riding of the County of York. Volume 1*, William Crofts, London.

Chadwick, E. (1842) *Report on the Sanitary Condition of the Labouring Population and On Its Means of Improvement*, London.

Challands, H. (1978) *A Demographic Study of Crosthwaite Parish; Some Genetic Implications*. Doctoral thesis, University of Durham.

Channing, L.H. (1985) Records of an English Church of Christ 1669 - 1842. [Tottlebank]. In http://www.fivenine.co.uk/family_history_notebook/source_extracts/parish_registers/lancashire/tottlebank_records_1.htm. Wembley Church of Christ, Wembley.

Chin, T. and Welsby, P.D. (2004) 'Malaria in the UK: past present and future', *Postgraduate Medical Journal*, 80, 663-666.

Christison, R. (1863) 'President's address in the public health department of the Social Science Association', *The British Medical Journal*, 2, 437-445.

Coleridge, H. (1851) *Poems by Hartley Coleridge with a Memoir of His Life by His Brother, Volume 1*, Edward Moxon, London.

Coleridge, S.T. (1817) *Sibylline Leaves, a Collection of Poems*, Rest Fenner, London.

Coley, W. (1785) *An Account of the Late Epidemic Ague Particularly as it Appeared in the Neighbourhood of Bridgenorth in Shropshire in the Year 1784; With a Successful Method of Treating It*. Printed for the author and sold by J. Murray, London.

Collingwood, W.G. (1903) 'On some ancient sculptures of the devil bound', *Transactions of the Cumberland and Westmorland Antiquarian and Archaeological Society, Series 2, 3*, 380-389.

Collingwood, W.G. (1906) 'Late and magic runes in Cumberland', *Transactions of the Cumberland and Westmorland Antiquarian and Archaeological Society, Series 2, 6*, 305-312.

Comrie, J. (1927) *History of Scottish Medicine to 1860*. Published for Wellcome Historical Medical Museum by Bailliere, Tindall and Cox, London.

Craig, T. (1876) 'On supposed lake or river terraces near Kelso', *History of the Berwickshire Naturalists' Club*, 7, 190-192.

Cranston, P.S., Ramsdale, C.D., Snow, K.R. and White, G.B (1987) *Keys to the Adults, Male Hypopygia, Fourth Instar Larvae and Pupae of the British Mosquitoes (Culicidae) with Notes on their Ecology and Medical Importance*, Freshwater Biological Association, Ambleside.

Crawford, P. (1984) 'Katherine and Philip Henry and their children: a case study in family ideology', *Transactions of the Historic Society of Lancashire and Cheshire*, 133, 39-72.

Creighton, C. (1894) *A History of Epidemics in Britain. Volume 2, From the Extinction of Plague to the Present Time*, Cambridge University Press, Cambridge.

Curwen, J.F. (1900) *Kirkbie-Kendall*, Titus Wilson, Kendal.

Danabalan, R. (2010) *Mosquitoes of Southern England and Northern Wales: Identification, Ecology and Host Selection*, Doctoral Thesis, Canterbury Christ Church University.

Danabalan, R., Monaghan, M.T., Ponsonby, D.J. and Linton, Y.M. (2014) 'Occurrence and host preferences of *Anopheles maculipennis* group mosquitoes in England and Wales', *Medical and Veterinary Entomology*, 28, 169-178.

Davidson, A. (1892) *Geographical Pathology. An Inquiry into the Geographical Distribution of Infective and Climatic Diseases*, D. Appleton and Co., New York.

Davies, O. (1996) 'Healing charms in use in England and Wales 1700-1950', *Folklore*, 107, 19-32.

Day, J.P. (1915) *Cambridge County Geographies. Clackmannan and Kinross*, Cambridge University Press, Cambridge.

De Quincey, T. (1854) *Autobiographic Sketches*, Ticknor and Fields, Boston.

Dibdin, C. (1802) *Observations on a Tour Through Almost the Whole of England and a Considerable Part of Scotland, in a Series of Letters, Addressed to a Large Number of Intelligent and Respectable Friends. Volume 2*, G. Goulding, London.

Dickens, C. (1868) 'Ague and its causes', *All the Year Round*, 19, 606-610.

Dickinson, W. (1852) 'On the farming of Cumberland', *Journal of the Royal Agricultural Society of England*, 13, 207-300.

Dickinson, W. (1859) *A Glossary of the Words and Phrases of Cumberland*, Callander and Dixon, Whitehaven.

Dickinson, W. (1875) *Cumbriana or Fragments of Cumbrian Life*, Whittaker and Co, London.

'Dick Summer's' (1805) 'Poetry for the Lancaster Gazette'. *Lancaster Gazette*, 5 October, p.4.

Dixon, J. (1783-1822) *General State of the Whitehaven Dispensary for the years (1783-1822), Annual Reports*, Whitehaven.

Dobson, M.J. (1980) '"Marsh Fever" – the geography of malaria in England', *Journal of Historical Geography*, 6, 357-389.

Dobson, M.J. (1989) 'History of malaria in England', *Journal of the Royal Society of Medicine. Supplement No. 17*, 82, 3-7.

Dobson, M.J. (1994) 'Malaria in England: A geographical and historical perspective', *Parassitologia (Rome)*, 36, 33-60.

Dobson, M.J. (1998a). 'Death and disease in the Romney Marsh area in the 17th to 19th centuries', In *Romney Marsh: Environmental Change and Human Occupation in a Coastal Lowland*. (Eds. J. Eddison, M. Gardiner and A. Long,), pp. 166-181, OUCA Monograph 46.

Dobson, M.J. (1998b). 'Marshlands, mosquitoes and malaria', In *Contours of Death and Disease in Early Modern England*. (Ed. M.J. Dobson), pp. 287-367. Cambridge University Press, Cambridge.

Duncan, K. (1993) 'The possible influence of climate on historical outbreaks of malaria in Scotland', *Proceedings of the Royal College of Physicians Edinburgh*, 23, 55-62.

Duncan, S.R., Scott, S. and Duncan, C.J. (1992) 'Time series analysis of oscillations in a model population: the effects of plague, pestilence and famine', *Journal of Theoretical Biology*, 158, 293-311.

Durham, H.E. (1901) 'The campaign against ague', *The British Medical Journal*, 1, 512-513.

Eccles, A. (1989) 'Vagrancy in late eighteenth century Westmorland: a social profile', *Transactions of the Cumberland and Westmorland Antiquarian and Archaeological Society*, Series 2, 89, 249-262.

Ewart, W.O. (1902) *The Climates and Baths of Great Britain: Being the Report of a Committee of the Royal Medical and Chirurgical Society of London. Volume 2*, MacMillan and Co., London.

Fahy, T.G. (1964) 'The Philipson family. Part 1, Philipson of Calgarth', *Transactions of the Cumberland and Westmorland Antiquarian and Archaeological Society*, Series 2, 64, 151-212.

Farrer, W. and Brownbill, J. (1914) *A History of the County of Lancaster, Volume 8*, London.

Fessler, A. (1950) 'A medical contract from the eighteenth century', *British Medical Journal*, 2, 1112-1113.

Findler, G. (1968) *Folk Lore of the Lake Counties*, Dalesman Publishing Co., Clapham.

Finlay, M.D.L. (1978) *An Enquiry into 'The Ague' in Scotland*, MD thesis, University of Edinburgh.

Finlay, M.D.L. (1980) 'An enquiry into 'the ague' in Scotland', *History of Medicine*, 8, 29-33.

Forbes, D. (1836) 'Cause and diminution of ague', *The Lancet*, 26, 527-528.

Forbes, T.R. (1971) 'Verbal charms in British folk medicine', *Proceedings of the American Philosophical Society*, 115, 293-316.

Ford, R.J. and Fuller-Maitland, J.A. (1931) *John Lucas's History of Warton Parish (compiled 1710-1740)*, Titus Wilson, Kendal.

Fordyce, G. (1795) *A Second Dissertation on Fever; Containing the History and Method of Treatment of a Regular Tertian Intermittent*, J. Johnson, London.

Franklin, P. (1983) 'Malaria in medieval Gloucestershire: an essay in epidemiology', *Transactions of the Bristol and Gloucestershire Archaeological Society*, 101, 111-122.

'G.W.' (1600) *Newes out of Cheshire, Concerning the New Found Well, as it is Contained in a Letter Lately Sent from a Cheshire Man, to a Gentleman a Deere Friend of His in Northampton-shire*, F. Kingston for T. Man, London.

Gambles, R.A. (1993) 'The spa resorts and mineral springs of Cumbria', *Transactions of the Cumberland and Westmorland Antiquarian and Archaeological Society*, Series 2, 93, 181-195.

Garnett, F.W. (1912) *Westmorland Agriculture 1800-1900*, Titus Wilson, Kendal.

Gill, C.A. (1921) 'Malaria in England with special reference to the role of temperature and humidity', *Journal of Hygiene*, 19, 320-332.

Gill, C.J. (2015) '*Plasmodium vivax* malaria in the UK', *British Medical Journal Online*, *BMJ2015;350:h1840doi:10.1136/bmj.h1840*.

Gough, G. (1789) *A History of the People Called Quakers from Their First Rise to the Present Time*, Robert Jackson, Dublin.

Gough, J. (1827) *The Manners and Customs of Westmorland and the Adjoining Parts of Cumberland, Lancashire, and Yorkshire*, Hudson and Nicholson, Kendal.

Gowland, R.L. and Western, A.G. (2012) 'Morbidity in the marshes: using spatial epidemiology to investigate the skeletal evidence for malaria in Anglo-Saxon England (AD410-1050)', *American Journal of Physical Anthropology*, 147, 301-311.

Gowling, M.E. (2011) *The Story of Brough Under Stainmore*, Hayloft Publishing Co., Stainmore.

Graham, H.G. (1899) *The Social Life of Scotland in the Eighteenth Century*, Adam and Charles Black, London.

Grierson, W. (1839) 'Ninth annual report of the proceedings of the Glenkens Society for improving the condition of the working classes', *Quarterly Journal of Agriculture*, 10, 384-426.

Gutch, E. and Peacock, M.G.W. (1908) 'Examples of printed folk-lore concerning Lincolnshire 63', *Country Folk-lore*, 5, 123.

Halliwell, J.O. (1847) *Dictionary of Archaic and Provincial Words, Volume 2*, John Russell Smith, London.

Harland, J. (1858) *The House and Farm Accounts of the Shuttleworths of Gawthorpe Hall, in the County of Lancaster at Smithils and Gawthorpe, from September 1582 to October 1621. Parts 3 and 4*, Manchester, The Chetham Society.

Harland, J. and Wilkinson, T.T. (1867) *Lancashire Folk-Lore: Illustrative of the Superstitious Beliefs and Practices, Local Customs and Usages of the People of the County Palatine*, Frederick Warne and Co., London.

Harris, W. (1762) *Historical and Critical Account of the Life of Oliver Cromwell, Lord Protector of the Commonwealth of England, Scotland and Ireland*, A. Millar, London.

Healey, J. (2008) 'Socially selective mortality during the population crisis of 1727-1730: evidence from Lancashire', *Local Population Studies*, 81, 58-74.

Henderson, W. (1879) *Notes on the Folk-lore of the Northern Counties of England and the Borders*, The Folk-lore Society/W Satchell, Peyton & Co., London.

Heysham, J. (1779-1789) *Observation on the bills of mortality in Carlisle for the years 1778-1788*, Printed by J. Milliken, Carlisle.

Hodgkinson, R.G. (1967) *The Origins of the National Health Services and the Medical Services of the Poor Law 1834-1871*, Publications of the Wellcome Historical Medical Library, New series 7.

Hodgson, E. (1937) *Glimpses of Witherslack*, Titus Wilson, Kendal.

Hodgson, J. (1810) *A Topographical and Historical Description of Westmorland, Containing an Account of its Towns, Castles, Antiquities etc.*, Sherwood, Neely and Jones, London.

Hodgson, J. (1825) *A History of Northumberland. Part 2, Volume 1*, J.B. Nichols, London.

Holt, J.S. (2011) *The Diary of Thomas Fenwick Esq. of Burrow Hall, Lancashire, and Nunriding, Northumberland, 1774 to 1794*, List & Index Society, Kew, Surrey.

Homan, P.G. (2006) 'Daffy: a legend in his own preparation', *The Pharmaceutical Journal*, 277, 783-784.

Hopkins, T. (1839) 'Observations on malaria with suggestions for ascertaining its nature', *The London and Edinburgh Philosophical Magazine and Journal of Science*, 14, 104-121.

Howson, W.G. (1961) 'Plague, poverty and population in parts of north-west England', *Transactions of the Historical Society of Lancashire and Cheshire*, 112, 29-55.

Hutchinson, R.A. and Lindsay, S.W. (2006) 'Malaria and deaths in the English marshes', *The Lancet*, 367, 1947-1951.

Hutchinson, W. (1794) *The History of the County of Cumberland and Some Places Adjacent*, P. Yollis, Carlisle.

Jackson, C.E. (1877) *Yorkshire Diaries and Autobiographies in the Seventeenth and Eighteeenth Century. Volume 1*, Andrews and Co., Durham.

Jackson, R. (1809) 'Dr Jackson's remarks on cobwebs', *The Medical and Physical Journal*, 22, 369-370.

James, S.P. (1929) 'The disappearance of malaria from England', *Proceedings of the Royal Society of Medicine*, 23, 82-97.

Jones, G.P. (1971) 'A short history of the manor and parish of Witherslack to 1850', *Cumberland and Westmorland Antiquarian and Archaeological Society Tract Series*, 18, 1-84.

Jones, J. (1700) *The Mysteries of Opium Reveald*, Richard Smith, London.

Keeble, T.W. (1997) 'A cure for the ague: the contribution of Robert Talbor (1642-81), *Journal of the Royal Society of Medicine*, 90, 285-290.

Kendall, W.B. (1948) 'The history of the hamlet of Salthouse', *Proceedings of the Barrow Naturalists Field Club*, 6, 21-40.

Kilgour, A. and Galen, J. (1842). Report of the sanitary conditions of the poor in Aberdeen, In (Ed. Anon.) *Reports on the Sanitary Condition of the Labouring Population of Scotland*, pp. 286-302. HMSO, London.

King, S. (2001) *A Fylde Country Practice. Medicine and Society in Lancashire, circa 1760-1840*, Centre for North-West Regional Studies, Lancaster University, Lancaster.

Kuhn, K.G., Campbell-Lendrum, D.H., Armstrong, B. and Davies, C.R. (2003) 'Malaria in Britain: past present and future', *Proceedings of the National Academy of Sciences*, 100, 9997-10001.

Lang, W.D. (1918) *A Map Showing the Known Distribution in England and Wales of the Anopheline Mosquitoes, with Explanatory Text and Notes*, British Museum (Natural History), London.

Lang, W.D. (1920) *A Handbook of British Mosquitoes*, British Museum (Natural History), London.

Leatham, I. (1794) *General View of the Agriculture of the East Riding of Yorkshire and the Ainsty of the City of York, with Observations on the Means of its Improvement*, W. Bulmer and Co., London.

Leigh, C. (1700) *The Natural History of Lancashire, Cheshire and the Peak in Derbyshire*, John Nicholson, London.

Levack, B.P. (2001) *New Perspectives on Witchcraft, Magic and Demonology. Volume 5*, Taylor and Francis, London.

Lewis, S. (1840) *A Topographical Dictionary of Wales Comprising the Several Counties, Cities, Boroughs, Corporate and Market Towns, Parishes, Chapelries and Townships with Historical and Statistical Descriptions,*. S. Lewis and Co., London.

Lewis, W. (1844) *A Topographical Dictionary of Scotland, Comprising the Several Counties, Islands, Cities, Burgh and Market Towns, Parishes and Principal Villages, Volume 2*, S. Lewis and Co., London.

Lindsay, S.W. and Joyce, A. (2000) 'Climate change and the disappearance of malaria from England', *Global Change and Human Health*, 1, 184-187.

Lindsay, S.W. and Thomas, C.F. (2001) 'Global warming and risk of vivax malaria in Great Britain,'. *Global Change and Human Health*, 2, 80-84.

Lindsay, S.W., Hole, D.G., Hutchinson, R.A. and Willis, S.G. (2010) 'Assessing the future threat from vivax malaria in the United Kingdom using two markedly different modelling approaches', *Malaria Journal*, 9, http://www.malariajournal.com/contents/91/70.

Linton, E.L. (1864) *The Lake Country*, Smith, Elder and Company, London.

Linton, Y.-M., Smith, L. and Harbach, R.E. (2002) 'Molecular confirmation of sympatric populations of *Anopheles messeae* and *Anopheles atroparvus* overwintering in Kent, southeast England', *European Mosquito Bulletin*, 13, 8-16.

Linton, Y.-M., Lee, A.S. and Curtis, C. (2005) 'Discovery of a third member of the *maculipennis* Group in SW England', *European Mosquito Bulletin*, 19, 5-8.

Lofthouse, J. (1953) *Lancashire Westmorland Highway with Byways and Footways for the Curious Traveller*, Robert Hale Limited, London.

Long, G. and Porter, G.R. (1849) *The Geography of Great Britain. Part 1. England and Wales*, Robert Baldwin, London.

Longstaffe, W.H.D. (1854) *The History and Antiquities of the Parish of Darlington, in the Bishopric*, J. Henry Parker, London.

Lonsdale, H. (1870) *The Life of John Heysham, MD and His Correspondence with Mr. Joshua Milne Relative to the Carlisle Bills of Mortality*, Longmans, Green and Co., London.

Loudon, I.S.L. (1981) 'The origins and growth of the dispensary movement in England', *Bulletin of the History of Medicine*, 55, 322-342.

MacArthur, W. (1952) 'A brief history of English malaria', *Transactions of the Royal Society of Tropical Medicine and Hygiene*, 46, 359-366.

MacCulloch, J. (1828) *An Essay on the Remittent and Intermittent Diseases, Including, Generally, Marsh Fever and Neuralgia*, Longman, Rees, Orme, Brown and Green, London.

MacKenzie, W. (1841) *The History of Galloway from the Earliest Period to the Present Time. Volume 2*, John Nicholson, Kirkudbright.

Magrath, J.R.E. (1904) *The Flemings in Oxford, Being Documents Selected from the Rydal Papers. Vol. 1, 1650-1680*, Oxford Historical Society at the Clarendon Press, Oxford.

Magrath, J.R.E. (1913) *The Flemings in Oxford, being Documents Selected from the Rydal Papers. Vol. 2, 1680-1690*, Oxford Historical Society at the Clarendon Press, Oxford.

Mannex, P.J. (1849) *History, Topography and Directory of Westmorland and Lonsdale North of the Sands in Lancashire*, Simpkin, Marshall and Company, London.

Markham, G. (1623) *Countrey Contentments, or the English Husewife*, R. Lackson, London.

Marshall, J.D. (1958) *Furness and the Industrial Revolution: An Economic History of Furness (1711-1900) and the town of Barrow (1757-1897)*, J. Milner, Barrow in Furness.

Marshall, J.D. (1967) *The Autobiography of William Stout of Lancaster 1665-1752*, Manchester University Press, Manchester.

Martineau, H. (1854) *Guide to Windermere*, John Garnett, Windermere.

Martineau, H. (1855) *Guide to the English Lakes*, John Garnett, Windermere.

Mason, R.W. (1867) 'Correspondence: Celtic etymology', *Archaeologia Cambrensis*, 13, 292-299.

Mason, S. (1745) *The Nature of an Intermitting Fever and Ague Considered*, J. Hodges, London.

Maynard, F.P. (1894) 'The prevention and cure of ague by opium', *The British Medical Journal*, 1, 437-438.

Medlock, J.M. and Vaux, A.G.C. (2011) 'Assessing the possible implications of wetland expansion and management on mosquitoes in Britain', *European Mosquito Bulletin*, 29, 38-65.

Meshnick, S.R. and Dobson, M.J. (2001) 'The history of antimalarial drugs'. In *Antimalarial Chemotherapy: Mechanisms of Action, Resistance and New Directions in Drug Discovery* (Ed. P.J. Rosenthal), pp. 15-25, Humana Press, Totowa, New Jersey.

Mitchell, G.A.G. (1939) 'Earlier medical history of Aberdeen', *The British Medical Journal*, 1, 336-338.

Morton, R. (1692) *Pyretologia Sive Tractus de Morbis Acutis Universalibus Variis Historiis Illustrata*, Perachon and Cramer, Geneva.

Muirhead-Thomson, R.C. (1956) 'Field studies on the role of *Anopheles atroparvus* in the transmission of myxomatosis in England', *The Journal of Hygiene*, 54, 472-477.

Nelson, P. (1937) 'Hale Hall glass', *Transactions of the Historic Society of Lancashire and Cheshire*, 89, 117-118.

Newman, L.F.and Wilson, E.M. (1951) 'Folk-lore survivals in the southern Lake counties and Essex: a comparison and contrast', *Folklore*, 62, 252-266.

Nicholls, A. (2000) 'Fenland ague in the nineteenth century', *Medical History*, 44, 513-530.

Nicolson, A. (2012) 'Unpacking the library of a 17th-century yeoman farmer reveals the rich inner lives of an ordinary family.' http://www.telegraph.co.uk/history/9134271/ Britains-original -information-revolution.

Nicholson, C. (1861) *The Annals of Kendal: Being an Historical and Descriptive Account of Kendal and its Environs*, Whittaker and Co., London.

Nuttall, G.H., Cobbett, L., and Strangeways-Pigg, T. (1901) 'Studies in relation to malaria: I. The geographical distribution of *Anopheles* in relation to the former distribution of ague in England', *The Journal of Hygiene*, 1, 4-44.

Ormerod, G. (1819) *The History of the County Palatine and City of Chester, Volume 2*, Lackington, Hughes, Harding, Mavor and Jones, London.

Page, D. (1875) *Report on the Sanitary Condition of Kendal*, Thompson Brothers, Kendal.

Page, H.A. (1877) *Thomas de Quincey: His Life and Writings*, Scribiner, Armstrong and Co, New York.

Palmer, W.T. (1905) *The English Lakes*, Adam and Charles Black, London.

Palmer, W.T. (1914) *Odd Yarns of English Lakeland*, Skiffington and Sons, London.

Paul, J.B. (1922) *Diary of George Ridpath, Minister of Stitchel 1755-1761*, T. and A. Constable Ltd, Edinburgh.

Philip, A. (1895) *The Parish of Longforgan. A Sketch of its Church and People*, Oliphant, Anderson and Ferrier, Edinburgh.

Picton, J.A. (1865) *Notes on the South Lancashire Dialect*, Privately published, Liverpool.

Porter, J. (1876) *History of the Fylde of Lancashire*, W. Porter and Sons, Fleetwood and Blackpool.

Prevost, E.W. (1905) *Supplement to the Glossary of the Dialect of Cumberland with a Grammar of the Dialect by S. Dickson Brown*, Henry Frowde and Bemrose and Sons Ltd., London.

Proudfoot, T. (1822) 'Topographical pathology of Kendal and its neighbourhood', *Edinburgh Medical and Surgical Journal*, 18, 374-392.

Quayle, T. (1812) *General View of the Agriculture of the Isle of Man with Observations on the Means of its Improvement*, W. Bulmer and Co., London.

Ramsdale, C.D. and Gunn, N. (2005) 'History of and prospects for mosquito-borne disease in Britain,' *European Mosquito Bulletin*, 20, 15-31.

Redding, C., Beard, J.R. and Taylor, W.C. (1842) *An Illustrated Itinerary of the County of Lancaster*, George Routledge, London.

Reiter, P. (2000) 'From Shakespeare to Defoe: malaria in England in the Little Ice Age', *Emerging Infectious Diseases*, 6, 1-11.

Relph, J. (1794) *An Inquiry Into the Medical Efficacy of a New Species of Peruvian Bark, Lately Imported Into This Country Under the Name of Yellow Bark*, James Phillips, London.

Rigby, E. (1783) *An Essay on the Use of the Peruvian Bark in the Cure of Intermittents*, J. Johnson, London.

Risse, G.B. (2005) 'Ague in Eighteenth-Century Scotland?: the shifting ecology of a disease', *Clio Medica: Studies in the History of Medicine and Health*, 171-197.

Ritchie, J. (1920) *The Influence of Man on Animal Life in Scotland: a Study in Faunal Evolution*, Cambridge University Press, Cambridge.

Robertson, E. (1911) *Wordsworth and the English Lake Country*, D. Appleton and Co., New York.

Robertson J. (1799) *General View of the Agriculture in the County of Perth: with Observations on the Means of its Improvement*, The Board of Agriculture, Perth.

Robins, A. (1864) *Black Moss. A Tale by a Tarn*, Richard Bentley, London.

Rollinson, W. (1974) *Life and Tradition in the Lake District*, J.M. Dent and Sons, London.

Ross, R. (1897) 'On some peculiar pigmented cells found in two mosquitos fed on malarial blood', *British Medical Journal*, 2, 1786-1788.

Sallares, R. (2006) 'Role of environmental changes in the spread of malaria in Europe during the Holocene', *Quaternary International*, 150, 21-27.

Sanders, R.A.N.S. (1771) *The Complete English Traveller; a New Survey and Description of England and Wales*, J. Cook, London.

Sandford, G.B. (1849) 'An account of the parish of Church Minshull in Cheshire', *Proceedings of the Historic Society of Lancashire and Cheshire*, 2, 85-113.

Saunders, W. (1792) *Observations on the Superior Efficacy of the Red Peruvian Bark in the Cure of Agues and Other Fevers*, J. Murray, London.

Scott, D. (1899) *Bygone Cumberland and Westmorland*, William Andrews and Co, London.

Scott, S. and Duncan, C.J. (1996) 'Marital fertility at Penrith 1557-1812: evidence for a malnourished community', *Transactions of the Cumberland and Westmorland Antiquarian and Archaeological Society, Series 2*, 96, 105-114.

Scott, S., Duncan, S.R. and Duncan, C.J. (1998) 'The interacting effects of prices and weather on population cycles in a preindustrial community', *Journal of Biosocial Science*, 30, 15-32.

Scott, S.H. (1904) *A Westmorland Village. The Story of the Old Homesteads and "Statesman" Families of Troutbeck by Windermere*. Archibald Constable and Co., London.

Sellers, R.F. (1987) 'Possible windborne spread of myxomatosis to England in 1953', *Epidemiology and Infection*, 98, 119-125.

Shirley, E.P., Dinley, T. and Prendergast, J.P. (1856) 'Extracts from the journal of Thomas Dineley Esquire, giving some account of his visit to Ireland in the reign of Charles ll,' *The Journal of the Kilkenny and South-East of Ireland Archaeological Society*, 1, 170-188.

Shute, P.G. (1945) 'Malaria in England', *Public Health*, 58, 62-65.

Shute, P.G. (1954) 'Indigenous *P. vivax* malaria in London believed to have been transmitted by *Anopheles plumbeus*,' *Monthly Bulletin of the Ministry of Health Laboratory Service*, 13, 48-51.

Shute, P.G. and Maryon, M. (1974) 'Malaria in England past, present and future', *Perspectives in Public Health*, 97, 23-29.

Sinclair, J. (1791-99) *The Statistical Account of Scotland Drawn up from the Communications of the Ministers of the Different Parishes*, Donaldson and Guthrie, Edinburgh.

Skirving, R.S. (1873) 'On the agriculture of East Lothian, with special reference to the progress made during the last twenty-five years', *Transactions of the Highland and Agricultural Society of Scotland*, 5, 1-48.

Smith, J.R. (1839) *Dialogues, Poems, Songs and Ballads by Various Writers in the Westmorland and Cumberland Dialects*, John Russell Smith, London.

Snow, K. (1998) 'Distribution of *Anopheles* mosquitoes in the British Isles', *European Mosquito Bulletin*, 1, 9-13.

Snow, K. (1999) 'Malaria and mosquitoes in Britain: the effect of global climate change', *European Mosquito Bulletin*, 4, 17-25.

Snow, K. and Medlock, J. (2006) 'The potential impact of climate change on the distribution of mosquitoes in Britain', *European Mosquito Bulletin*, 21, 1-10.

Southey, C.C. (1850) *The Life and Correspondence of the Late Robert Southey. Volume 8*, Longman, Brown, Green and Longman., London.

Sparke, A. (1917) *The Registers of the Parish Church of Deane. Burials 1604:1613-1750*, Lancashire Parish Register Society, Bolton.

Stockdale, J. (1872) *Annales Caermoelenses or Annals of Cartmel*, William Kitchin, Ulverston.

Sydney, M. (2009) *Bleeding, Blisters and Opium. Joshua Dixon and the Whitehaven Dispensary*, Stainburn Publications, Whitehaven.

Talbor, R. (1682) *The English Remedy or Talbor's Wonderful Secret for Cureing of Agues and Feavers*, J. Wallis, London.

Taylor, S. (1955) *Cartmel People and Priory*, Titus Wilson, Kendal.

Trappes-Lomax, R.E. (1930) *The Diary and Letter Book of the Rev. Thomas Brockbank*, Chetham Society, Manchester

Tyrer, F. and Bagley, J.J. (Eds.) (1968-1972) *The Great Diurnal of Nicholas Blundell of Little Crosby 1669-1737*, The Record Society of Lancashire and Cheshire, Liverpool.

Virgoe, J. (2005) 'Causes of mortality in a rural south-west Lancashire community in the late eighteenth century', *Journal of Local Population Studies*, 75, 33-55.

Walford, T. (1818) *A Scientific Journey through England Wales and Scotland. Volume 2*, J. Booth, London.

Wallis, J. (1769) *The Natural History and Antiquities of Northumberland; and of so Much of the County of Durham as Lies between the Rivers Tyne and Tees*, W. and W. Strahan, London.

Ward, J.E. (1998) 'Death in eighteenth century Whitehaven: the records from Holy Trinity Church', *Transactions of the Cumberland and Westmorland Antiquarian and Archaeological Society*, Series 2, 48, 249-261.

Warter, J.W. (1850) *Southey's Common Place Book. Series 4. Edited by His Son in Law*, Longman, Brown, Green and Longmans, London.

Waugh, E. (1892) *Lancashire Sketches*, John Heywood, Manchester.

Webster, C. (1868) 'On the farming of Westmorland', *Journal of the Royal Agricultural Society of England*, 4, 1-38.

Wheeler, A. (1802) *The Westmorland Dialect in Four Familiar Dialogues,*. M. Braithwaite, Kendal.

White, W. (1859) *Northumberland and the Border*, Chapman and Hall, London.

Whitfield, D., Curtis, C.F., White, G.B., Targett, G.A., Warhurst, D.C. and Bradley D.J. (1984) 'Two cases of *falciparum* malaria acquired in Britain', *British Medical Journal (Clinical Research Edition)*, 289, 607.

Whitley, G. (1864) *Residence in Marsh Districts*, Eyre and Spottiswood, London.

Wilkinson, T.T. (1861) 'On the popular customs and superstitions of Lancashire', *Transactions of the Historic Society of Lancashire and Cheshire*, 13, 1-15.

Williamson, T. (2006) 'The disappearance of malaria from the East Anglia fens', *International Journal of Regional and Local History*, 2, 109-122.

Wilson, C. (1841) 'Statistical observations on the health of the labouring population of the District of Kelso in two decennial periods, from 1777 to 1787 and from 1829 to 1839', *Proceedings of the Border Medical Society*, 1, 47-85.

Winchester, A.J.L. (1994) *The Diary of Isaac Fletcher of Underwood, Cumberland, 1756-1781*, Cumberland and Westmorland Antiquarian and Archaeological Society, Kendal.

Womersley, D. (2009) 'Dean Swift hears a sermon: Robert Howard's Ash Wednesday sermon of 1725', *The Review of English Studies*, 60, 744-762.

Wordsworth, W. (1888) *The Complete Poetical Works by William Wordsworth*, McMillan and Co., London.

Wright, T. (1880) *Dictionary of Obsolete and Provincial English. Volume 2*, George Bell and Sons, London.

Wrottesley, F.J. (1906) *Trentham Parish Register 1558-1744. Volume 1*, Printed privately for Staffordshire Parish Register Society.

Index